100 TYPES OF MEN TO AVOID

DATING FUNNEL
FOR WOMEN
How to Spot Bad Boys & Filter Them Out Quickly

ESRA OZ

INGI, LLC

Published by: INGI, LLC

https://esraozdenerol.com/

http://www.datingfunnelforwomen.com/

ABOUT THE BOOK

Are you tired of constantly attracting the wrong type of men? Do you feel like you're stuck in a never-ending cycle of bad relationships? Look no further than "**Dating Funnel for Women: How to Spot Bad Boys and Filter Them Out Quickly; 100 Types of Men to Avoid.**" A genuine eye-opener for the single woman who repeatedly asks, "Is he Mr. Right?"

Dating Funnel for Women is not your ordinary dating book! It teaches a simplistic dating approach, going on multiple dates with a variety of men and filtering out the high value one, who is offering you the solidity, maturity, and adulthood you need for life partnership. Author Esra Oz reveals the 100 types of men you should avoid that will break your heart, waste your years, and make you miss opportunities with the high value man you wish would love you and commit to you. **Dating Funnel for Women** will change the way you think about dating, the relationship process and ultimately yourself. You will immediately gain a powerful abundance mindset, confidence with men, relationship understanding and an attractive, intriguing presence. This book creates a profound paradigm shift empowering women in their dating journey.

ABOUT THE AUTHOR

Esra Oz, commonly known as Dr. Esra Oz, is an author, coach, and the creator of **datingfunnelforwomen.com. "The Dating Funnel Journal"** accompanies her book "**Dating Funnel for Women: How to Spot Bad Boys and Filter Them Out Quickly; 100 Types of Men to Avoid"**.

She empowers single women to ditch the dating struggle and claim the loving relationship they so deeply deserve. She teaches a simplistic dating approach, going on multiple dates and filtering out the high-value man, who is offering you the solidity, maturity, and adulthood you need for life partnership.

You can also join her social media community **"Dating Funnel for Women"** on Facebook and/or Instagram for tips on dating and how to create a dating funnel. She developed an easy-to-follow guide on identifying and avoiding the types of men who are not worth your time. For more tips on how to date with more intention and less stress, listen to her podcast **"Dating Funnel for Women"** on Spotify and Apple Podcast. She also offers live group coaching on a rotating schedule and 1:1 coaching. Check out the website **www.datingfunnelforwomen.com** to see when the next session begins, explore the master class, and download a dating funnel blueprint as a reference for your dating journey and follow me on Instagram **@dresraoz**.

Table of Contents

Dating funnel

Dating funnel is not your ordinary dating book! It teaches a simplistic dating approach, going on multiple dates with a variety of men and filtering out the high value one, who is offering you the solidity, maturity, and adulthood that you need for life partnership. After all, dating is a filtering system for knowing who is truly right for you. Funneling helps you intuitively avoid the wrong men who will break your heart, waste your years, and make you miss out on opportunities with the high value man whom you wish would love you and commit to you. This book spells out 100 types of men who you'll know about how to filter their low value behaviors while funneling, - who he is, how he will lure you in and how you will spot him before you are hooked.

Whether through online dating or meeting organically, you pour all the new men you meet into your man funnel. Fill the top of the dating funnel with prospective men whom you would like to go on a date with. Your goal is to increase the number of men going into your funnel. By keeping your options open in your man funnel, you meet more men and have a better chance of finding the right one who will step up and claim you as his, ready to give you what you want. When you meet lots of men, you put less focus on any one man. This will keep men interested by simply giving them space to be curious of your life. This will also prevent you from investing far too much in the first decent man you meet, even if he's far from being the right one. Abundance leads to confidence.

At this stage, it is about meeting new people and getting to know them. Every interaction with another human being is a possible gateway to some new world or experience, which could, in turn, introduce you to the love of your life. In this group, there will be men who may seem attractive at first glance, but you don't have any immediate chemistry; there will be ones you have chemistry with, but not compatible with you; there will be high value men who are not a good match for you, and there will be the ones you are genuinely interested in spending time with. You will experience men who are clear, confident, imperfect but genuine and focused on what they want - they make it clear, no games. There are extraordinary people everywhere, but it will take some filtering to find that certain someone who fills your needs and desires.

Dating in the modern world requires being smart and savvy. The smarter you get filtering them out, the closer you will be to meeting the right one. You don't have all the time in the world and all the room in your heart for heartbreak by giving yourself to a man before you know he is the right choice for you. You take your time making sure that his character, his investment in relationships, his integrity and his heart matches your heart and values and that it is right. During the funneling process, you will also date a string of the wrong men who will come to you in sheep's clothing but inwardly are ravenous wolves. You will recognize these wolves spot on and filter them out quickly.

Adopting an easy come and easy go attitude will let you gain a powerful abundance mindset, confidence with men, relationship understanding and an attractive, intriguing presence that will magnetically attract not only the sincere interest of quality men, but a quality life.

Below are the little nuggets of wisdom you pick up while funneling:

> Gives you options and empowers you.
> Let you enjoy dating and recognize the love of your life.
> Let you meet more men and have a better chance of finding the right one.
> Allows you to put less focus on any one man who will stimulate his curiosity on you.
> Prevents you from investing far too much in the first decent man you meet who is not the right one.
> Let you compare the competition of pursuing men.
> Helps you find out more of your likes and dislikes.
> Helps you pause for clarity.

- Gives you thinking opportunities that are crucial to making intelligent decisions.
- Helps you gain a new perspective and look at a situation with fresh new eyes.
- Helps you not to get sucked into a fantasy relationship.
- Helps you cultivate honesty and vulnerability.
- Helps you be aware of their flaws and hidden motives.
- Avoids the major pitfalls that leave you sad, lonely, and wasting critical years.
- Helps you grow in self-awareness; it effects how well you perform in your dating life.
- Let you spend the time needed for self-reflection.
- Helps recognizing emotional triggers and makes you open to learning from your mistakes.
- Allows you to have a much greater chance of seeing the situation clearly.
- Let you pause to pray. Pause to ponder. Pause, so you can avoid the pitfalls.
- Seeks god's wisdom.
- Seeks the counsel of wise people.
- Waits for the universe's direction.
- Brings you lightness, and flow.
- Allows you to have much more fun than linear dating.
- Helps you learn how to attract and choose the RIGHT man.
- Truly evaluates if there's a good match and find out what's missing in your connection.
- Sets the bar high.
- Allows you to be strong-minded and confident in who you are, and what you have to offer.
- Helps in meeting fresh prospects, making your dating life exciting and eliminates scarcity thoughts.
- Let you have realistic expectations.
- Helps you in getting to know who you really are.
- Is much healthier for your wellbeing.

Mr. Right

At first glance, he seems like Mr. Right. He sweeps you off your cynical feet with nice dinners, roses, thoughtful gestures. The sex is incredible. You want to introduce him to your mom. But before you fall hook, line, and sinker-stop! He could be one of these 100 dating mistakes…

Some men are master anglers. Once you're hooked, you'll invest your love, soul, money, and possibly, valuable childbearing years before realizing – too late – that they aren't your real happily ever after. In the end, they'll break your heart, shatter your ego, and frustrate the heck out of you. Though these bad boys may be hard to spot, they send out subtle clues that they're a relationship hazard. Read on for the 100 types of men to avoid…

1

Mr. Ghoster

Who he is: Going out with this man is like dating Casper, the friendly ghost. He is pleasant and personable, but an emotionally immature ghost child. He is anxious in love, difficult to settle into or get comfortable in a relationship. He senses that you want commitment; suddenly, he would vanish *poof* - the communication comes to a screeching halt. This could happen at the very beginning of a relationship or in the middle of one, as well as in person or online and painfully in a serious relationship that lasted in a significant period. You usually don't know the cause or know how to react, feeling humiliated and confused.

How he'll lure you in: At first, he seems super interested in you. You've established communication, regular lines of contact. He will do everything in his power to impress you. He may even brag and lie, trying to be someone he is not. He makes promises that he can't keep. More time passed, and you notice that you were always the one reaching out and initiating any kind of communication.

Spot him before you're hooked: If he ghosts you, respect the dead and refrain from reaching out. It's not your responsibility to change his decision. Avoid waiting for an explanation; closure comes from letting go and believing in better opportunities. If he tries to return, ignore him and move forward as if his message never reached you.

2

Mr. Scammer

Who he is: He is a con artist, expert at what he does and will seem genuine, caring, believable and too perfect! He is not looking for love. He could be an overseas criminal phishing for your private information using a fake online identity. He often says that he is engaged in projects outside the country. He preys on lonely women.

How he'll lure you in: He will establish a relationship as quickly as possible, endear himself to you, and gain trust. He will quickly ask you to leave a dating service or social media site to communicate directly. He will romance you, propose marriage and make plans to meet in person, but that will never happen. Eventually, he will ask for money for a medical emergency, unexpected legal fee or invest in cryptocurrency.

Spot him before you're hooked: Be cautious if he seems too good to be true. Go slowly and ask lots of questions. Beware if he promises to meet in person, but then always comes up with an excuse that he can't. Avoid falling victim to this type of crime. Stop communicating with him immediately.

3

Mr. Liar

Who he is: This guy's all about lies. He is a compulsive liar with very low self-esteem, and he lies to make himself feel better. In public, he will constantly try to get attention by telling strangers his war stories, his cancer defeat, his professional and academic accomplishments. He will wear you out with the endless chatter about him being this great person. He will ruin the possibilities of your relationship by betraying your trust. When he is idle, he takes selfies and texts them to other ladies online for attention.

How he'll lure you in: He's putting forth a "lot of effort" to show you a good time, but really it is to give himself a good time. He will get your attention with his manipulative tactics and lies. He lies about little things that never even mattered. He makes up stories, even when it would be just as easy to tell the truth.

Spot him before you're hooked: You will notice early on that a few things were not matching up from previous conversations. You will recognize flagrant lies. You will wonder what else is a lie? Are you safe with him? Be sensitive to his dishonesty and manipulative tactics. Go no contact with him; it is the best thing you can do.

4

Mr. Marry-Go-Round

Who he is: Mr. Marry-Go-Round is eager to go ring shopping. He's not afraid of commitment, in fact, getting married is on his agenda. He seems over the moon excited and feels so lucky to marry you. When the romance is gone, he will quickly move on to a younger wife. Dumping his wives is as easy as trading his cars.

How he'll lure you in: He is head-over heels gaga with you. You are immediately dazzled, and a torrid, intense romance begins. He will be sprinting down the aisle and introducing you as the future Mrs. So-and-So. Once the lovey-dovey honeymoon phase is over, Mr. Marry-Go-Round will blame you and make you soon realize that his love towards you is not as solid. He doesn't take marriage seriously, he is simply unequipped to handle the adversity which comes with a marital relationship, so he dissolves the marriage rather than working on it.

Spot him before you're hooked: One divorce is understandable, as are two divorces with good reasons. Four divorces indicate a pathology. Find out exactly how many times he's been married. If he'll soon outpace Larry King – and his brides are getting younger – that should stop, you or at least make you pause.

5

Mr. Peter Pan

Who he is: Mr. Peter Pan is an irresponsible 30 or 40 - something frat boy, who never got past his college partying phase and shows up to work hungover and hooks up to experience intimacy. He is always ready for fun. Though, his playfulness works against involvement in life's difficult situations. He is going to disappear every time your life gets a little complicated.

How he'll lure you in: It is all fun and games for him. You will party hard every weekend. He has a boyish charm. His cheerful spontaneity brings out the kid in you. He's the one who persuades you to ditch work for an afternoon at the ballpark or the beach.

Spot him before you're hooked: You will find yourself acting more like a parent than a girlfriend. He'd ask for back rubs and eat your kid's Lucky Charms. The more you give, the less he does. Sticking around will only result in heartbreak and resentment of his inability to grow up.

6

Mr. Confirmed Bachelor

Who he is: Mr. Confirmed Bachelor is smart, charming, successful. He will sweep you off your feet, and you expect to get married six months later. At first, he seems a stable, reliable life companion but his interest is only expanding his dating pool to take his pick.

How he'll lure you in: He plays the role of eligible bachelor and tells you that he just hasn't found Mrs. Right yet. You will feel like you've found a good catch, you could be her. You will soon realize he has been part of the scene for years. There is no right woman, and you will not be the one.

Spot him before you're hooked: Actions and deeds speak louder than his lovey dovey words. He doesn't see the point in introducing you to his friends and family. He will always keep some distance between you so that things don't get too serious. His past relationships last only a few weeks or a few months at most. If he hasn't gotten married by the time he's 50, he's probably not going to tie the knot.

7

Mr. Emotionally Unavailable

Who he is: The conversation flows smoothly when it's about friends, plans for dinner, or your clothing choice. However, when you start sharing more emotionally about your family, or discuss your plans for your future, he checks out. He has a difficult time knowing how to engage in the real-stuff conversations. He will use sarcasm as a defense mechanism and resort to laughter and cut himself off emotionally from you.

How he'll lure you in: He is so sweet and engaging and thoughtful, that you give it a shot. You will be wondering where the man you loved went. Unfortunately, this was who he was the whole time. He just hid it "well" at first. His past remains a mystery to you, and you will never get to know him on a deeper level.

Spot him before you're hooked: When you would like to take your relationship with him to the next level and get serious, he will want to remain unattached. You may have a feeling of stagnation where the good isn't growing and the love is not deepening. He never lets his guard down around you to say what's really on his mind. You will never know his fears, insecurities, hopes, and dreams. You wish he trusts you and feels safe opening up to you. Wishful thinking!

8

Mr. Just Texter

Who he is: He sends daily texts to you. Days go by, sometimes weeks go by, but he never asks you out. He keeps his text buddies on the line while he decides if he wants to meet any of them. It's obvious that he's not interested in making plans with you.

How he'll lure you in: The conversation is creative, funny, and exciting. He keeps up the flirting and texting because it gets his ego boost. He is content experiencing your feminine energy without ever needing to date you.

Spot him before you're hooked: You will soon figure out he is not serious when you take the lead and suggest talking on the phone or meeting. Make the decision for him. Stop answering his texts and move on. He is not worth your precious time.

9

Mr. Narcissist

Who he is: He wants you to believe he's the best possible person you could date or the only person who would put up with you. He has excessive need for admiration; he may do almost anything to achieve those ends, no matter how cruel. He will use you for personal gain and when you're no longer of use to him, he will discard you. He will turn vicious, vindictive, hateful, and void of any empathy for you.

How he'll lure you in: He makes you feel unique. The first few months, even years, are a whirlwind of romantic dinners, getaways, and heady conversations of how you're soulmates to each other and perfect for each other. In fact, he's testing to see if you will be a good source of narcissistic supply.

Spot him before you're hooked: He will try to isolate you from friends and family. He will manipulate you to such an extent that you eventually doubt your own perception. You'll find yourself feeling confused, anxious, depressed, and scrambling to be good enough. Do not let him define your identity and your worth. You dodged a bullet and you're better off moving on. The best way to move on is "no contact."

10

Mr. Toxic

Who he is: He demands respect, but does not have any left for you. He does not care what is important to you. He'd make fun of you, ridicule you, and maybe even bully you. He does whatever he wants. He becomes aggressive, wants to intimidate you, and may even become physical. He loves to flip the narrative; it's always everyone else in his life who is the problem, never him!

How he'll lure you in: He moves too fast in a relationship. He will want to get serious quickly without getting to know you first. He acts overprotective and smothering. Most of the time in the relationship is spent doing sexual things. He waits for you to solve the problems.

Spot him before you're hooked: They might show up uninvited to your home or office, borrow things without asking, invade your personal space, or make decisions without consulting you first. You know very well that he is not good for you. You only give, but get nothing in return. He imposes the work on you. Love becomes pure poison if you stay with him. He brings you nothing but heartache and grief. Please, just dump his ass!

11

Mr. Wonderful-But-Broke

Who he is: He looks for the financially well-off woman so that he can mooch off of her. He gets to know about your family to learn about your wealth. He has champagne tastes on a beer budget. His closet is a financial burial mound. He has a supernatural ability to get into your wallet as well as your bed. He will never be an equal and worthy partner in the equation.

How he'll lure you in: His indomitable spirit and joy for life are what lures you in. He'll play on your natural affinity for nurturing and care taking. He encourages you to persevere in pursuit of your dreams so that you could be the breadwinner forever and he would continue being nobody as he calls it "he's his own boss."

Spot him before you're hooked: Whenever it's time to pay, he left his wallet at home or he's short on cash until he gets paid. Initially, it might seem reasonable to float him a little extra. One day, you may find yourself buying him a car, co-signing on a loan, or making a down payment on a house. He'll try to convince you that "it's for our future." Leave him before he puts you deep in debt and tanks your credit rating.

12

Mr. Mama's Boy

Who he is: He couldn't survive alone out in the wild without his mother. His mom always knows about everything. He lets his mom spoon-feed him and run every decision for him. His mom cannot do anything wrong. And if you say otherwise and push him to choose sides, you will be on the losing side!

How he'll lure you in: He is great in romancing you. He's sweet, affectionate, and understanding. You think you finally met someone who cares about how women feel and knows how to treat a woman until you realize that you are competing for his affection with his mother.

Spot him before you're hooked: He might as well still live at home. By dating him, you are basically committing to his mother. He compares you to his mother – and you come up short every time. At the most intimate level of his heart, he still loves Mom as much or more than you, cut him loose.

13

Mr. Egomaniac

Who he is: He's the macho guy, who exudes confidence with a tad bit of aggression. He is outgoing, demanding, and very sexist! He tends to be very boastful about his accomplishments, loves tooting his own horn, and constantly shows off. There's no give and take, just his lecturing and condescending attitude. After all, God made him perfect, and the world revolves around him.

How he'll lure you in: He's brilliant, accomplished, and decisive. You never see him waffling or agonizing about a decision. He's got that Clint Eastwood, John Wayne, macho inner strength, and confidence that's really appealing to you. He is also easier to approach and talk to. When that confidence crosses the line and turns into egotism and superiority, it can quickly turn unappealing.

Spot him before you're hooked: He surrounds himself with minions, but has few real friends. He doesn't care what you have to say. He may listen, but only long enough to prepare for his next persuasive statement. He might embarrass you at an office party or run you down in front of colleagues in the guise of "being funny." When you complain, he'll accuse you of being too sensitive. He is not only rude and snappy to you, but to waiters, cabbies, housekeepers, the parking lot operator, the barista, and so on. You will soon be turned off by his arrogance. Keep your distance!

14

Mr. Control Freak

Who he is: Dating with this man is suffocating. Mr. Control freak not only asks all the questions, but he also answers them all too. He believes that if he is not holding your hand, you are going to screw it up. He will eventually dictate everything from what you wear to how you spend your free time.

How he'll lure you in: At first, he may have come off as thoughtful, warm, and secure. But before long, you will be gasping for air. All this attention is certainly flattering. After all, he must really love you if he's so concerned about you, takes such care of you, and wants to be with you all the time, right?

Spot him before you're hooked: He plans all your dates and tells you how to dress or act around his friends. He expects you to agree with him, and if you don't, he tries to convince you that you're wrong. He will ask frequent status reports and attempts to control each moment of your time. He will become overly focused on who you spend time with when you are not with him. Once you realize that he's trying to get you to be who you're not, run – don't walk away.

15

Mr. Gaslighter

Who he is: He is into crazy making! He tells lies consistently and will deny it when you call him out on it, even if you have proof. He is the master manipulator and shares common traits with extreme narcissists. He intentionally manipulates you to make you think that you are going crazy by making you have a false sense of reality.

How he'll lure you in: All his attention is certainly flattering. He shows that he is so concerned about you. First, he will give you a compliment or encouragement then put you down, and you end up being confused. He uses your confusion to his advantage because he knows it makes you weaker.

Spot him before you're hooked: It is not one behavior you can point to, but a bunch of lies and manipulation that add up over time. You spend every conversation talking in circles, being told that why you're always at fault, apologizing for anything he did wrong, and feeling like a piece of human trash. You get so sick of dealing with his manipulation, you stay silent instead of expressing your emotions. If you often get confused around this person and don't know why, because he is gas lighting you. Before he turns you to question your own sanity, it is time to get out of this relationship!

16

Mr. Scandalmonger

Who he is: This man will gossip indiscreetly to a level that he spreads malicious gossip about you and others. He is quick in trashing you and your friends or the people whom he considers better than him. He suffers from an inferiority complex. It's very hard for him to keep a secret. If you break up, he will use your secrets against you, either to force you into something that he wants or just to blackmail you for nothing.

How he'll lure you in: Most surprisingly, at first, his gossiping skills will strengthen your dating and create more bonding and intimacy. He gossips with you about other people and you foolishly assume that he does not talk to others about you. When he has more knowledge and control of your information, he has more status. He will ask you more personal questions and as you become more open and honest, you think that you are building a deep, personal and trustworthy connection.

Spot him before you're hooked: He reacts in a way that undermines the trust and confidence that you put in him, and he uses what you tell him against you when you fight. You find yourself confiding less and less in him; sharing less and less; in general, just not offering information with him from the heart because you fear that everything you say will be used against you at some point in the future. Better cut him off or set boundaries for your own self. Focus on saving yourself from this guy or your secrets get passed down the grapevine until everyone knows!

17

Mr. Breadcrumber

Who he is: He leads you on with no real intention of developing a relationship. He is all about games. He leaves a trail of 'crumbs' of attention or affection to give you hope and sees you coming back for more, which makes him feel wanted and worthy. He has narcissistic tendencies, craving your attention to feel powerful and special, actually giving nothing in return.

How he'll lure you in: He is overly affectionate from the start. He showers you with compliments and physical affection, only to start taking them away once you are hooked. You get that mad rush of feelings and butterflies straight away and romanticize this relationship and exaggerate the worth of the breadcrumbs.

Spot him before you're hooked: You never know where you stand with him. He could already be in a relationship with someone, and yet, is still seeking attention from you. Set healthy boundaries. Maintain your social activities so that you're not dependent on the breadcrumber. Engage in self-care and don't let him play with your self-esteem and emotions.

Mr. Married Dater

Who he is: He might tell you that he is separated and will be getting a divorce, often trying to play victim in his divorce case, and tries his best to get as much sympathy as he can. He often uses this strategy to be with another woman, or he straight up lies that he is legally married to get you to agree to sex. He wants short-term emotional or physical gratification rather than true love from you.

How he'll lure you in: At first, he will wine and dine you. He possesses the qualities of a high value married man—more mature, responsible, and caring, which often forms the basis of getting attracted to him. Compliments from him may seem more flattering as you get more attracted to him. You often become empathetic towards him when he discusses his dissatisfactory married life, especially his sex life, and the sad stories of his ungrateful, complaining, annoying wife, as he titles her.

Spot him before you're hooked: If he withholds his real name, lacks transparency, and only spends time based on his availability, leading to anxiety and neglect, be aware. If he swiftly cuts contact when caught by his wife, prioritize yourself—ditch him for a man who values exclusive devotion. Recognize your worth; don't settle for someone treating you as just another option. Get wise before it's too late.

19

Mr. Player

Who he is: He is a fragile boy who once got hurt and never got to recover from it. He tries to avoid getting hurt at all costs. He's not looking for commitment, but will 'play' games to make you think that he is. He doesn't have consideration towards your feelings and will tell you anything it takes to 'play' you into bed, making you feel like his toy.

How he'll lure you in: You hear everything that you ever wanted to hear. You notice that he's giving lots of compliments or getting physically close, but he's not asking you questions about yourself or engaging in conversation. He's the nicest and kindest when he's around, but does not notice you when he accidentally runs into you somewhere out in public.

Spot him before you're hooked: He barely reaches out to you, and when he texts you, you notice him constantly trying to make it about sex. He's almost desperate to lead the conversation towards sexting. He reaches out to you, only when you both have to meet up, which is always at his place or yours, or anywhere where it is only the two of you. He always finds good excuses not to stay over after 'the fun time' is done. That is the purpose of his flattery; and when that's done, there's no reason left for him to be with you anymore. There is no point dating him. He is only looking for a good time and not a genuine connection. He is a waste of your time and emotions.

Mr. Divorcee Sloth

Who he is: His divorce had been horrendous, leaving him gun shy about another serious relationship. He is slow to make decisions and reluctant to make an effort. After the divorce, he'd resolved to keep his children separate from his dating life. He made sure that he was at his kids' sports games and band concerts. Even after a considerable time of dating, he still would keep you away from his family and friends.

How he'll lure you in: You can't get enough of cheek kisses, hand holding, hugs, and an arm around you. He's likely had a lack of those things for a while. All this attention is certainly flattering. He wants to be adored, but doesn't want to be smothered. He only opts for cute gestures in the beginning to act as nice as a gentleman as he can.

Spot him before you're hooked: You empathize with him, but it hurts to have a critical part of his life ruled off-limits to you. You will try to change the situation and feel less in limbo about things. He will continue to put his family first. He sees it as being a step towards a more serious or permanent relationship, which he is not yet ready for. Someone who really loves you would want to share the joy with their family and loved ones and not hide you from them, nor keep it a secret. Instead, he would be proud to have you by his side. He is confused with his plan for the future, and that probably won't work for you. Move on!

21

Mr. Astrodater

Who he is: If you're wondering how your astrological sign plays into your dating life, Mr. Astrodater will choose the best date idea for your zodiac sign. This intellectual astrology wizard searches for true compatibility. He talks about the horrific details of his past dating lives and refuses to date a specific astrological sign ever again. He does not give attention to your individual personality traits more so than your zodiac sign.

How he'll lure you in: First date, he will check his astrological compatibility with you. Through your conversations, he will be able to guess your zodiac sign correctly. He will romance you based on planets. Based on his astrological predictions, you are the most compatible couple and best lovers.

Spot him before you're hooked: He is super into horoscopes. Every time you got into an argument or had any banal disagreement, it would be filtered through the lens of Zodiac. Everything is fixed in the stars, and no one ever had any legitimate real-world motivations for their behavior. If you can't work to mutually understand each other better and grow in your compatibility without his astrological predictions, you better stay clear of this astrology wizard.

22

Mr. Executive Type

Who he is: He is a high achiever, focused on his career. He's likely to want to put all his energy into that. He expects to see you only on his terms, whenever and wherever it's convenient for him because he has a busy schedule. His brain is so good at the rational stuff but when it comes to the emotional stuff, he finds it difficult. You need to create dedicated time when you don't talk about work. All his life revolves around work and success, and you are just another person in his life who he likes and that's it.

How he'll lure you in: He is smart, powerful, charismatic, and very successful. You admire his charm and charisma. You will get to go to any restaurant you want and attend a lot of social events. Dating an executive is more about quality time vs. quantity. He knows how to give a girl a good time. His personality and grace charms you to fall for him.

Spot him before you're hooked: Your dates are going to be interrupted by phone calls, emails, and sometimes even cancelled altogether – at the last minute. You feel like you're not a priority and it can cause a huge number of arguments. He still must ask you out in advance, and you must turn him down politely if he expects to see you only on his terms; otherwise, he will take you for granted. It does NOT matter if he is a CEO with respect and lots of power and money, he must act like a partner to you. Your happiness should always come first.

23

Mr. Traveling Businessman

Who he is: He is a traveling businessman who wants a girlfriend in every city. He dates around and meets new people without getting too attached. *"I'll be in town for work. Just looking for some casual fun"*. He wants an emphasis on 'No strings attached'. His excuse is *"I don't get back here often"*. He's not looking for a serious relationship. He wants to date you, but other women as well at the same time.

How he'll lure you in: At first, you respect him because he wants to take a small, gradual approach in dating his partner. He is so relaxed because of his casual approach. You have some fun without all the complications and drama of dating with expectations.

Spot him before you're hooked: His approach is more centered on sexual gratification and being open. There is no pressure to introduce you to his world. He thinks serious relationships are high maintenance, whether romantic dates, taking vacations, or attending family gatherings, you're expected to do things as a couple. He can simply walk away when things get tough or when he is not interested anymore. Simply, he can come and go as he pleases without all the fuss. He is lame, skeezy, and not remotely worthy of your time.

24

Mr. Friends-With-Benefits

Who he is: He does not want to hook up and sleep around with just anyone, but prefers to hook up with friends without really dating each other so that he doesn't feel obligated. He has the peace of mind that there is less drama and demands on him. He is basically an irresponsible punk who would rather have fun.

How he'll lure you in: You enter an FWB because you want to sow your wild oats. You can explore and experiment with many things. FWB gives you all the freedom in the world like one-night stands, flings, or whatever you want. There is no commitment to anybody and your friend with benefits can't get jealous because they understand the deal. Even if the other party is not cool with it, you can both easily move on by ending things with no hard feelings.

Spot him before you're hooked: The major source of headache in FWB is that someone always ends up wanting much more than what was originally agreed upon. You can start developing deeper feelings that ultimately lead to complications. It is easy to forget about safe sex when regularly having sex with him. True feelings may not be involved, but still the other party might be hurt. It takes a lot of energy and maturity to handle more than one friend with benefit; so if you are going for more than one, be ready for all the work.

25

Mr. Reminding You-of-Your Ex

Who he is: He reminds you of your ex that you had a difficult relationship with. He feels familiar and you naturally gravitate towards him. You may find yourself being attracted to men of a problematic type, whom some way, you'd like to go back and fix, or simply, to try your luck one more time with a modified model of the previous product.

How he'll lure you in: His looks and personality remind you of your ex. You find yourself highly attracted to him because this feels familiar. The level of discomfort with him sharing a name and similar traits directly correlates to how your ex made you feel. You lose a lot of sleep thinking about what to call him and how to save his number in your phone.

Spot him before you're hooked: You're likely to keep dating people just like your ex, despite how bad of a relationship it was. If you find yourself deliberately looking for someone like him, you are not over your ex. If you're running into the same type of face/person, that's not about love and fate, it's about an unresolved issue in your past that keeps you codependent on rewriting that story in hopes that it will turn out to be the one. You should consciously know to stay away from dating certain types of men that are wrong for you.

26

Mr. Sports Fanatic

Who he is: He is all into watching and talking sports and won't pivot to what you are interested in; sounds like he's self-centered. His date ideas are always about watching sports. He has energy, but it is directed to the game. It only works so long as you jump on-board and cheer with him. He will make you feel sorry for his paranoid self when he had to hang out with you instead of watching his favorite team. He spends money on sports bets and takes his team very seriously. His mood on the weekend is entirely dictated by the outcomes of games that he's irrationally invested in.

How he'll lure you in: His pickup line is "Did you see the game last night?" The game is a major conversation topic in the days following your meeting. He offers to help you with your fantasy football league. Time spent on the couch watching ESPN releases bonding chemicals in his brain and you both love spending time together watching your favorite team – in the beginning.

Spot him before you're hooked: Beware! His ideal date involves watching games at home or chilling with friends for fantasy football, beer, and junk food. No fancy dinners—potato skins are more his style. If you can't handle the "It's just a game" mindset, steer clear; he's emotionally invested in his team. On the upside, choosing a birthday gift is a breeze—just grab two team jerseys like your nephew wants.

27

Mr. Hobbyist

Who he is: He prefers to build his relationships around his hobbies and passions: restoring houses, cars, art, forming new businesses, traveling internationally, playing golf, fishing, hunting, four-wheeling, gaming, BBQ competition, etc. He spends countless hours and money on his hobby that brings only temporary gratification and TO HIM ONLY. He doesn't realize the damage that he does to his dates. Coupling with him leads to separate lives, with hobbies that take the place of conversation and connection.

How he'll lure you in: You most likely meet him in the off season, help him prepare his gear. At first, you find it very attractive when he is passionate about his work/hobby/art. You can't help but "admire" and look up to him who is very invested in something because he enjoys it so much. You find it a unique and valuable trait and, therefore, are attracted to him.

Spot him before you're hooked: His dates will never come before his "hobbies." He will spend all year preparing for the one season of fishing, hunting or barbecue competition. Once the season is over, the cycle continues. When it comes to your interests, however, he seems to space out and generally, does not care. You get to determine over time, if you are content with the effort that he's putting into your dating life. Putting golf or gaming before the relationship? Stay single. Demanding you take up four-wheeling? Dump him immediately.

28

Mr. Pervert

Who he is: He will send you unsolicited cock pics and caption it with pride: "See, what you are missing?" He has a sense of pride in knowing that his penis can generate a strong reaction from you. He will ask you about your cup size and request nude photos. Don't be surprised to find out that he is a professional, middle-aged man, whom has a wife and kids.

How he'll lure you in: He talks about him being horny, makes you think that he desires you and wants you badly sexually and develop intimacy with you. He generates sexual excitement, leading to some sexting and, you know, naughty stuff being sent over the phone lines. His intent could be a joke or to shock you when he sends his cock pics to reciprocate nude pictures of you.

Spot him before you're hooked: He is overtly sexualized. He is testing to see if you are easy or loose. Forget courting and flowers, his method of flirtation is communicating his sexual desire via an image of his genitals. No way that this is the first time he's done this. Such behavior is infantile. Such men neither have any self-respect nor do they know how to respect others. You can send him a yawn emoji and the word PASS and block him.

29

Mr. Workaholic

Who he is: He thrives on work. The idea of leaving for a vacation throws him into a panic. He feels anxious, agitated, and distant. He does feel guilt, at times, about neglecting you and the social events that you invited him to, but he refused without a second thought. He appreciates not being nagged because he struggles to separate his dating life from work. He will often overbook his life, finding unexpected opportunities or problems challenging. He is a workaholic and does not have time for dating you.

How he'll lure you in: At first, you admire his determination to work hard. His ambition and energy attract you. He has an impressive resume and career aspirations. But soon, you realize that he works hard only at his job but not at his relationships.

Spot him before you're hooked: You don't want to be the one holding on to Mr. Workaholic, while he is flinging and prioritizing everything else before you. He cancels plans for dinner or social engagements. He will go on working and you will keep on getting hurt. Stop bothering and making date plans. He will either take out time for you, or dump him and seek out someone else who values quality '*us time*' than '*his time*' and go from there. You will be shocked how easy it is to do things with someone else who prioritizes you!

30

Mr. Long Distance

Who he is: He tells you that he misses you and that distance sucks because you can't be together, but adds that you should keep your options open in the meantime. He genuinely likes you but still wants to play the field when you're not around and doesn't mind if another guy snatches you up. It's more like an open relationship which is not really a good connection in your love life.

How he'll lure you in: When you're together, he seems super into you. He talks about you to his friends, comfortable with engaging in a public display of affection, and compliments you all the time. He initiates every conversation, checks up on you if you don't reply, makes plans in advance, clears his schedule for you, and does all the polite things that need to be done in a nice, romantic relationship.

Spot him before you're hooked: He wants everything that's happening right now and nothing more. He is already happy with the status quo, and you're not going to get a different result just waiting around for something to change. He does want to keep talking. He does want to see you when he sees you. He says that he doesn't want an exclusive long-distance relationship with you, BELIEVE him! Hopeless expectations will take you nowhere with this kind of man, you deserve so much more than this.

Mr. In-Love-With-Coworker

Who he is: He is secretly in love with his co-worker. He might protect her real identity or have the audacity to tell you "You should dress like her." "You should do your hair like her." "Look how pretty she is." "Why doesn't your body look like that?" Not only do comparative comments like those have 'mega jerk' written all over them, but they are also letting you know that anytime you hear him talk about his female coworker, it's never truly in a platonic way. It's either about her looks, her intelligence, or her assets. He is making more of an effort to make her life easier at work than he is making any effort at his dates with you. He has lunch dates with his, "She's just a co-worker/she's just a friend". He goes to work trips, just her and him. He shares his personal problems, feelings, and thoughts with his co-worker instead of you.

How he'll lure you in: He prides himself in never having been a cheater, boasting and blabbering about it, often. Never once was he ever unfaithful to anyone. You have good sex, and you like hanging out and watching TV together. The intensity of your relationship grows equally, and you are proud to call him your man. You will soon discover his dark, sneaky, slick, and shady ways with his 'just a coworker'.

Spot him before you're hooked: If he claims they're just friends discussing work, don't entertain doubts. Avoid accusations to prevent arguments. Soon, she's having relationship problems with her boyfriend, so they've been talking about how she's thinking about leaving him. Despite her relationship issues, prioritize your feelings and insist on being his priority. Don't let comments about insecurity bother you; demand to be the one he puts first before other women.

32

Mr. Deadbeat Ass

Who he is: He can't hold down a job very long. He has no ambition, no motivation, no drive. He is a lazy bum, sleeping a lot and sleeping in. He has no problem consistently receiving money or items from you and others. He doesn't pay his debts or even acknowledge them. He doesn't respect money and thinks that it isn't important. He is surrounded by douche-bag friends. He plays video games endlessly. He is constantly losing or breaking his belongings. He has little or no respect for the time and effort it took to obtain them. To him, only survival is enough, and having a good lifestyle is just extra.

How he'll lure you in: When you first meet, you think that you found your prince charming and happily ever after! You fall prey to his sugar-coated words that melt you. He seems easy going and laid-back. His attention is flattering. You become sexual too quickly. Before you know it, you are in a co-dependent relationship with him.

Spot him before you're hooked: Avoid downplaying your hard work by dating him, where you end up doing the work of two or dealing with his laziness and its consequences. His lazy and irresponsible attitude will likely lead to irritation and frustration, causing a downward spiral. Don't tolerate feeling unloved—value yourself enough to deserve someone better than his deadbeat behavior.

33

Mr. Ungrateful

Who he is: He is just ungrateful and unappreciative for anything that you have done for him. He is a professional victim who assumes that others are supposed to take care of him. It is not his culture to thank others. He was taught to be polite and forgot. He will take you for granted and assume that you will understand that they are grateful. You are never enough for him.

How he'll lure you in: At first, he always wanted to spend time together. He was willing to do everything he could to make sure you were happy, and invest his time, effort, energy, and money into your dates.

Spot him before you're hooked: He pulls away. Problems don't get resolved; he is no longer interested in being invested in the relationship. It's probably because he doesn't feel like you are enough for him anymore. He becomes boorish and overly critical. 'You're a bitch who does nothing for me'. The criticism extends to the way you live, your job, your appearance, your family etc. And so, the cycle repeats - he'd make you feel guilty, demoralized, inferior and you would be endlessly innovative in an attempt to make him happy. He is always the victim. To continue to try to please this type of man serves only one purpose - to fuel his behavior. Stop giving, stop doing, stop being what you think he wants!

34

Mr. Minister

Who he is: Reformed wild child turned devout church member, he uses Bible verses to emphasize his points. A seemingly devout volunteer, he secretly imposes strict rules on women, especially those of faith, highlighting Ephesians 5 to enforce submission to men. Behind the spiritual facade, he's a controlling individual with a dirty agenda.

How he'll lure you in: He's always been religious like with his speeches to you on how he prides himself in being a family man with Christian values. He leans on his faith in God and sends you social media links and faith-based messages throughout the day. You grew up in church and have always been the "good girl." God put him in your life to share your faith and he is your destiny.

Spot him before you're hooked: Beware of the charming, good-looking churchgoer who initially appears perfect, but later reveals a mean streak. As your dates progress, you'll witness his anger drama, including belittling others and showing prejudice. Tearing down others seems to be in his DNA with the ultimate aim of saving your soul and turning you into a true believer. Save yourself the effort, release him back to God, and stop trying so hard for someone with such destructive behavior.

35

Mr. Alcoholic

Who he is: He is a recovering alcoholic who used to be a rock-star, partier, or wake and baker, who used to get high and drink every day. He is now a changed man and claims a successful recovery. In fact, he carries a deeply seated sense of shame in who he is and what he has done. He has more intense and wavering emotions at times. He still cannot function on his own and did not surrender for sobriety to happen. You attempt to rescue him from his issues.

How he'll lure you in: He is an inspiration for everyone around him with the success and perspective gained once sober. You feel empathy for him and show extra understanding and patience. You're tempted to help him become a better person for himself and in the process, you find yourself falling for him.

Spot him before you're hooked: While you should be a source of compassion and support, the decision to remain sober is your date's responsibility. Taking time to reflect on yourself will prevent you from folding under the weight of his serious financial troubles, a criminal record, or limited contact with his children or loved ones as a result of his addiction. Be aware of your own mental health status as well as his recovery process!

36

Mr. Pill Popper

Who he is: He can't get through the day without taking a cocktail of prescription drugs. He will display extended lethargy and drowsiness, but will also show signs of an elated mood as well, all because of his medications – the common effects of drugs.

How he'll lure you in: He is curious, creative, and imaginative. He is neurotic and has high openness to experience. You were attracted to his receptivity to new ideas and new experiences. The loving, kind, sweet act he puts on for you turns into low agreeableness, and he will use intimidation and aggression to get his own way.

Spot him before you're hooked: You may see this person starting to excuse himself from social events or maybe he doesn't ever return your calls. He changes his physical appearance quickly; he may go from showering every day to bathing every few days. He forgets about chores or duties. It's no surprise that you may have also noticed some of your cash has gone missing, or maybe a credit card. Watch out for missing medication as well. He puts on a convincing show of ignorance. This pattern of events may be far too regular to be random while dating him. His severe mood swings and aggression would become a problem for you. Stop lowering your expectations and devise ways to overlook his behavior!

37

Mr. Paranoid

Who he is: He still hurts over his ex's actions, and he believes that everyone is going to be out to get him. His lack of trust manifests in controlling and paranoid behavior. He's always looking out for that time where he's going to trip you up; he may never be able to move past it and forgive you. He will check your devices or ask other people about you. He won't ever learn to trust you, no matter how hard you try.

How he'll lure you in: He always thinks that he has been treated unfairly by women. You sympathize with him. He makes you believe that he couldn't live without you in the beginning. Having someone seem to be into you without question seems like a gift from God so you suck it up and become addicted to the high.

Spot him before you're hooked: He hasn't let go of the past, and this manifests in how he behaves with you. He re-lives and re-creates the past in his head. He struggles to communicate about things that upset him. This leads to resentment built up. He demands constant reassurance from you, which can become draining and exhausting. Regular expression of insecurities is annoying and exhausting. You have to clarify each and every smallest action in your life. Let him go! He's not in the right frame of mind to make it work and let alone, come out of the paranoia!

38

Mr. Fraudster

Who he is: He lives beyond his means and has financial difficulties. He believes that he is above the law and, therefore, can subvert it. He covers up financial felonies and misdemeanors. He may engage in criminal misconduct or was incarcerated for x number of years. His life has no honesty left for you to put your precious trust in him.

How he'll lure you in: He is a highly educated, intelligent man. He could be an attorney or a banker who has a "wheeler-dealer" attitude. He will impress you with the lifestyle he once had from the model of his car, square footage of his house, to the dollars in his bank account. He is attentive, caring, and affectionate. You sure won't know the tricks he has up his sleeve.

Spot him before you're hooked: He puts on a convincing show of a lifestyle he had. He still lives in the past and did not learn from his lessons. He'll twist the story; change the way it happened and retell it so convincingly that he'll believe his own nonsense. He'll lie before he ever apologizes. You will soon realize that he is knowingly doing bad deeds and not caring for you.

39

Mr. Vaper

Who he is: He is addicted to vaping and won't quit. He started vaping to cut back on his cigarette use. It's something to have in his hand and to be doing. If he's watching TV, he'll be vaping. If he's bored, he'll be vaping. If he is stressed, he will be vaping. Even if he's in a good mood, he'll vape. He does not make the effort for dating. The more he vapes, a lot more anxious he gets. He drains your energy.

How he'll lure you in: There is always a sweet scent in the air! He "probably" wouldn't have started vaping if it wasn't for that gummy bear flavor. You find his boyish good looks very attractive. He seems cool and nice at first. He is charismatic and laid back.

Spot him before you're hooked: His sole joy is blowing vape clouds, showing no interest in enjoyable activities or dates. His addiction, worse than cigarettes or alcohol, becomes overwhelming. He disrespects you, and vaping leaves a noticeable smell and residue. Stand up for your right to clean air, bid farewell to Mr. Vaper, and move forward in your dating journey for fun and enjoyable dates!

40

Mr. Gym Rat

Who he is: He is at the gym, ALL the time. He is an exhibitionist, self-obsessed, extremely vain, and very muscular. He shows off his big muscles. He spends all his money on protein and creatine, and on 3 brands of multivitamins and 2 brands of fish oils. This is the guy who will spend countless hours in front of the mirror, praising his so-called amazing, jaw-dropping looks and body. He has a weight scale for him and for his food. He is obsessed with body building.

How he'll lure you in: He will compliment your appearance or fitness level; it's definitely a sign that he's attracted to you. He may make small talk about your workout routine or what type of exercises you like to do. Healthy lifestyle and healthy living can definitely bring you two closer, just like a set of dumbbells that are always together. You dream of all the couple's workouts you can do with him.

Spot him before you're hooked: Your first date is at a gym or eating a salad, counting the macros. You like working out, but it's not your life - he goes to the gym 7 days a week. His dates will never come before his "workouts." The core problem with him is never what he looks like - it is how he feels about himself. He is "addicted" to the gym and extremely obsessed with his or your body and fitness. You respect his way of doing things and let your gym junky enjoy his salads!

41

Mr. Retired-Want-To Be

Who he is: He is dedicated to living frugally to retire far earlier than conventional retirement plans would permit. He openly tells his early retirement goal at your first date. This goal dictates his lifestyle and dating life to an extent that he evaluates every expense in the hopes to be able to quit his job.

How he'll lure you in: Surprisingly, he will show generosity and kindness at first. He will pay for dinner dates and give lots of affection. You have terrific physical chemistry and shared interests, but not shared values.

Spot him before you're hooked: If you allow him, he will eat breakfast, lunch, and dinner at your house until his beloved retirement and not contribute towards groceries. If the fridge goes bare, he will stop at the deli counter and get himself a sandwich and nothing for you. Draw a line in the sand. Stop fixing meals. Even though you tell him that your finances are tight, and you can no longer afford to feed him, he will just resent the reality check. Don't let him play guilt-trip games either. Healthy relationships are based on mutual give and take. He places himself before anyone else, and he won't get better. You have found yourself a freeloader, and better consider ditching him fast before he kills your finances…

Mr. Tag-Along-His-Kids-To-A-Date

Who he is: He will tag along his kids to a zoo date or walking through the pumpkin patch. Your date nights include watching Mickey Mouse Clubhouse while cleaning up toys. You even catch yourself drafting a text message from his phone, on his behalf, to his ex. You may feel like a stepmom long before everyone else considers you to be a stepmom.

How he'll lure you in: Blending into his family will be unlike anything you've ever experienced before, and it could be rewarding, especially if you don't have children. After all, he wouldn't introduce anyone to his children without having some intent to stay with that person and have a future with them. He just wants to know that his prospective date is able to cope with children and can shoulder their responsibility as their own.

Spot him before you're hooked: Introducing you to his children doesn't imply seriousness; it's a routine for him. He lacks intentionality in scheduling alone time, turning your relationship into more of a babysitting role. If you feel neglected, expect guilt-tripping and gaslighting. Take time to discern the intentions of anyone you're romantically interested in.

43

Mr. Fashion Police

Who he is: He has a flamboyant personality who gets all fashion police on you. He does not lose time to tell you that he doesn't love your fashion sense by criticizing your choice of outfits – "You can't wear that, it's showing too much". "I would want to see you in this shirt and this type of blazer". "You are overdressed". He does not say let's go shopping together and make it fun and engaging for both of you.

How he'll lure you in: He is eccentric. When he walks into a room, you notice him. He's a big personality and his dress sense reflects that. When you first got together, you noticed his flair with fashion straight away. You are attracted to him and his sense of style and his graceful aura. You like that he takes his time to look good for you, because that is what he says in every date.

Spot him before you're hooked: Small changes to your wardrobe choice are okay as long as the suggestions are within reason, and you feel that you can still maintain your own basic sense of style, that is a part of your personality. You listen to his thoughts and change your look when appropriate, to show how he feels is important to you. But if you have to adjust your wardrobe to his insecurities, jealousy, or a desire to be controlling, you will eventually resent him and put your foot down. Life is way too short to confine yourself to outfits that don't reflect who you are. Find someone who will accept you for who you are, not for what you wear.

Mr. Business Partner

Who he is: He is the guy you can't tell if he wants to talk business with you or wants to date you. He senses your entrepreneur spirit. You bring a unique set of gifts and ideas, enthusiasm, dedication, and devotion to your dating life. He gets on the idea of pursuing a business with you. He is too lazy to implement an idea and take the risk and stress of it all, but easy to give praise to your business ideas and risk-taking abilities. He starts talking about investing in stocks and real estate with you.

How he'll lure you in: At first, he is understanding and supportive. You believe in him, it's like he is giving you the wind beneath your wings. He likes to spend private time together to learn tiny details about your finances and business ideas, reinforced with a kiss or physical affection.

Spot him before you're hooked: He is eager to borrow money from you, use yours and your family's resources for his 'real needs', and he would make you believe that he will return the money. He could be hiding important financial information such as major debt, a bankruptcy, or a clear issue with excessive credit card usage. You are not in business together; take the business hat off and put the dating hat on. Just take your time to get to know the person. Stop oversharing and spilling sensitive details about your finances and business ideas to your date in the first go.

45

Mr. Hopeless Romantic

Who he is: He wears rose-colored glasses when it comes to potential love. His desire to have it is so strong that he's compelled to create it in his mind and with people with whom it doesn't exist. He often falls in love with the idea of someone and not the actual person. He love-bombs with manipulative demonstrations of devotion and false promises.

How he'll lure you in: There is emotional investment from day one. On the first date, he talks about marriage, romance, wedding venue, his dream honeymoon location, and such stuff. You venture into fantasy land with his fairytale script that he sends you with poems and songs and romantic sunset and kissing videos.

Spot him before you're hooked: Slow down! He has grand declarations of adoration and butterfly-inducing words that rival Romeo and Juliet. He establishes impractical expectations of you because he's measuring you against the image in his mind. He often uses gifts and romance to distract you from his other concerning behaviors, such as control and jealousy. He chases an emotional high so much so that he neglects his interests and hobbies and focuses on you and only you to a level that makes you uncomfortable. You need to give him a reality check that rarely matches his fantasies. Let him dream about you in his sleep and you seek a hopeful and intentional lover in real life!

46

Mr. Tonsil Hockey

Who he is: He has little self-awareness and control when it comes to sexuality. He is the guy who will strain your neck and tongue muscles while kissing. He does tonsil hockey thinking it is a sign of arousal for either party! He continues licking your face like a dog and still doesn't understand that you need to come up for air! You look for a lighthearted way to bring it up, so he does not get his feelings hurt or defensive.

How he'll lure you in: He loves pursuing and seducing you. He is attracted to you. He is respectful of your wants and needs. He is enthusiastic and affectionate to you. He makes it obvious with his words and mannerism that he wants to have sex with you.

Spot him before you're hooked: He is aggressive with his kisses. You lean back, slow the kiss, not give the chance to go deep, and he is still unaware of his drooling and sweat on you! It is better to show him than tell him that you prefer soft and gentle kisses and proper hair pulling techniques. *"I prefer we kiss lightly. May I show you how I prefer to be kissed?"* Hope he learns quickly. If it is hard to train him, and you never get used to his kissing, go on with your funnel!

47

Mr. Wanderlust

Who he is: He's struck with wanderlust. He is energetic and spontaneous. He is equipped with all the necessary gadgets. Be ready to spend the weekends outside of your comfy home. He is constantly on the go, posting breathtaking views of him backpacking at the other side of the world. He could be teaching English in China, building a home for someone else in the foreign wilderness, gliding down warm sand dunes with newly met friends, and jumping into clear lakes with local kids. He is eager to tell you everything about his work away experiences, and how much he misses you. Though, settling down is simply not part of his life plan. He will never be content with living a conventional life in one place.

How he'll lure you in: You like the fact that he is adventurous and spontaneous. You pack your bags for sudden plans, take unexpected roads, and explore untamed lands. You are not only attracted to the person but his free spirit, passion, and generosity. You already start fantasizing counting stars in a pollution-free sky, or just walking barefoot through nature with him. He never shies away from trying new things and not just romantic for special occasions!

Spot him before you're hooked: If he loves you as much as the world and wants shared adventures, consider planning work trips together. However, be cautious with a man leading a random, passionate, commitment-free life, maintaining love interests worldwide. Balancing such a lifestyle with a job and daily routine can be challenging, so carefully weigh the pros and cons before committing to a traveler-centric life.

48

Mr. Cougar Chaser

Who he is: He does not shy away from openly expressing his love interest in dating older women. He is with you just because he wants to see how it feels. His confidence with maturity is how he attracts older women. Having a fling with you is a sort of commitment for him and he actually has an irrational fear of commitment.

How he'll lure you in: Dating a younger man who is spontaneous, adventurous, and full of ideas might sound tempting at first. A young man brings more energy, enthusiasm, spontaneity, and fun to a relationship. You listen to your heart and give it a try! He does not let the spark die. He continues to surprise you with his unique, crazy ideas. Doesn't matter what the age is; women love surprises, right? He says that you are what matters, and not the number. He lets you know that age doesn't matter when it comes to love and meaningful connections and you two are sharing this beautiful equation because he wanted this to happen with you.

Spot him before you're hooked: If he's the right person and a match in heaven despite the age difference, prioritize shared values; however, if he constantly nags, lacks accountability, and his lifestyle differs significantly, consider letting him go, especially if his friends and family struggle to accept you.

49

Mr. Feminine

Who he is: He is the new Renaissance man, exhibiting sensitivity, culture, and fine taste for everything. He has a dapper suit, perfect hair, clean-shaven face, and manicured nails. He'll always want to dress to the nines and draw admiring stares. He can share a bottle of organic exfoliating wash and he'd be happy to go to the farmer's market with you. He is more open and expressive when it comes to his feelings. He's going to be strict with his diet and encourage you to do the same. He is effeminate, pushover and meek.

How he'll lure you in: He will cuddle with you while watching chick flicks together. He will share his collection of poems and songs. He's always so clean even prim and proper. Manscaped almost non-existent body hair, and even a slight touch of makeup. He'll even cook you paleo dishes, just so you can both stay healthy and fit. You enjoy dating him.

Spot him before you're hooked: Be prepared to buy those pricey beauty products for you two. Say goodbye to Marvel movies. Since he is as sensitive as you, he may even have his own PMS, at times, you have to tiptoe around him a lot of the time. You'll always have to watch what you say, because you don't want to hurt him. He can't open a jar of pickles. In fact, he's not handy at all. If a light bulb needs changing or a faucet gets a leak, you'll have to call a handyman, because all your guy is good at is manscaping. Before you brush off a feminine man as being too girly for you, consider what your priorities are.

50

Mr. Asexual

Who he is: He has little or no interest in sex. Flirting is not part of his personality. He prefers close friendships to intimate relationships. You may have a connection, but not in the bedroom. Sex will never be his priority, once every so often is enough for him. Even with that, he thinks that he is doing you a favor.

How he'll lure you in: You have a great emotional connection and friendship. He accepts you for who you are. He shows that he cares deeply for you by his actions. At first, you both enjoy cuddling and kissing. He takes things slow in a relationship. He is permissive in many ways.

Spot him before you're hooked: You don't have any physical contact aside from holding hands and cuddling on a rare occasion. You wonder is it a medical issue? Is he waiting for marriage? Your confusion turns into realization that he has a very low sex drive. Once you learn that they are asexual, don't try to change them. If you think that your dating life with this man is fulfilling even without sexual intimacy, he may be providing the companionship you may be looking for. But if this creates insecurity and becomes an issue for you, you need to step back and see if dating with this type of man is worth pursuing. You are incompatible in an area that is important to you ethically. It's okay to communicate and move on. Don't compromise your heart for company!

51

Mr. Obsessed-With-Politics

Who he is: He is obsessed with politics. He talks about the subject non-stop, watches political videos all day long. He goes on political rants about things he hears on the news or social media. He sends social media and text messages of political debates and conspiracy theories at odd times throughout the day. He does not consider and respect your priorities and concerns.

How he'll lure you in: At first, you find him very smart, intellectual, and down to earth. That leads to hours of nonstop talking about the world affairs, politics, your careers, your lives, everything! You have "real person" conversations that creates a connection between you two.

Spot him before you're hooked: He gets so worked up that things aren't enjoyable anymore. He becomes caught up in politics to the point of obsession. He wants the party candidate he backs to win so badly that he talks about almost nothing else. He even does not get over it after the election has been settled. You can't go anywhere without the politics being brought up. He doesn't have enough else going on in his life. It becomes hard to overlook. To keep the peace, you just let him rage. It gets boring and annoying with time. When you try to talk to him about it, he gets defensive. Please cancel your twitter account and filter him out quickly from your funnel rather than saying "it's just politics".

52

Mr. Loves-His-Naps

Who he is: He wants to sleep and nap every time you hang out. He sleeps through your dates and doesn't call you or pick up the phone when you call him. He doesn't make much effort to try and suggest other things to do when you see each other. He's lazy and needs a girlfriend just for the smallest part of his day when he can't sleep.

How he'll lure you in: He is very sweet, attentive, and caring... but... he sleeps through half of your dates. You have a desire to go out and explore with him, make memories together. But... you spend half your time waiting for him to wake up and the other half motivating and convincing him to join you for some fun.

Spot him before you're hooked: You're excited to see him and be spending quality time with him – only for him to fall asleep and leave you hanging. He would sleep anytime and anywhere, without caring about any of your plans or even emotions. He wouldn't cut 'his time napping' ever and would dig in to 'us time' to get his things done and claim that he is doing what you asked for. You should stop bothering and making plans and tell him that there's more to life than sleep!

53

Mr. Fantasy

Who he is*:* He is the guy who you fantasize and can't have. You are mentally stuck on him; you don't know how this man is like in a real relationship. Unfortunately, you've gotten it into your head that you'll never meet someone else like him.

How he'll lure you in: Your crush is imaginary and not about him. You are putting this person on a pedestal based on how you perceive the little of him you have seen. You think about him all the time, like a hopeless romantic. You're so drawn to his perfection as of the male protagonist of a romance novel.

Spot him before you're hooked: You mainly have feelings for a fantasy. There's a part of you that knows that fantasizing about him is a distraction from the vulnerability of actually dating. Be careful to never put him up on a pedestal anymore and catch yourself early. People are just humans, and everyone has their flaws. Staying grounded makes it much easier to truly get a feel for people and compatibility. Take it as a lesson on what you like, hold it as a standard. Stop looking at his social media or keeping in contact with him. Meeting somebody else in real life could help you let go of that fantasy. Put yourself out there!

54

Mr. Fisherman

Who he is: He is an angler, loves to go fishing. He posts his fish like his trophy. All he thinks about is fishing. His Zen-like focus is what makes him better at fishing. It is also why you hit a wall every time you try to steer him away from his finned friends.

How he'll lure you in: You feel special he shares his super-secret fishing spot with you at your first date. Perfect date for him is you two exploring up a creek with two poles waiting for a bite. For Mr. Fisherman, you sound like a real catch! You're attracted to his skills and focus.

Spot him before you're hooked: Don't come between him and his finned friends... Your summers are monotonous, controlled by his compulsive fishing. His obsession makes you feel lonely in the relationship when it's not supposed to be that way. There is no fun and fulfilling activity you do together rather than fishing. You try to learn to love fishing or learn to make your own plans without feeling resentment. Even though you compromise, he is not willing to budge a little and dedicate a weekend to you. You're either hooked on fishing, or let him chase his slimy finned friends for the rest of his life and continue on with your dating funnel.

55

Mr. Not-Over-His Ex

Who he is: He hasn't taken the time to heal and process his last relationship. He blames himself for the breakup in a way that seems like he'd change the past if he could. He isn't over his ex and still has an attachment to her. He tends to rush in a new relationship very quickly and attempting to recreate that experience with you.

How he'll lure you in: He takes you to super romantic dates. You start to hang out 24/7. He arranges last-minute getaways and meeting each other's friends. You feel almost drunk on the buzz. You've only known each other for a brief time but you are in a whirlwind romance.

Spot him before you're hooked: He can't kick the ex-habit. One minute, you hear idealization and fondness when he talks about his ex and sounds regretful. How good of a woman and a mother she was, nothing wrong with her, it is all on him. Another minute, he assigns blame, and gets worked up and angry. He puts on a good show most of the time, but he is still on the emotional mend. He's not ready for something serious. Trust, connection, and love are built over time so there is no need to rush. Take your time getting to know him to make sure he is who he appears to be. Don't hang your romantic hopes on him. Continue on your dating funnel and see other people, spend time with your friends and focus on filling your life in ways beyond him. Maybe you should believe him that there is something wrong with him to leave a good wife.

Mr. Recycler

Who he is: He tends to cycle through the same set of women who are willing to take him back repeatedly. He'd rather keep these women around who he can use periodically than having to start from scratch. He does not really care which of the women accompanied him, as long as he got whatever he wanted. He is not concerned about the feelings of these women. He walks out easily; he puts them on his recycling list and keeps it moving. He recycles places like he recycles women. When the place no longer serves his needs, he moves on. Then he comes back to the town. He blames long distance for not committing.

How he'll lure you in: Love bombing is his way of reminding you of the good old days. Once you start thinking about the way he used to make you feel in that brief time you dated, there is a high chance you will take him back. He likes his life to be spontaneous. When he decides it's time to win you back, he will start digging for information about you. He might send you a message on your birthday, the holidays, or the anniversary of your first date.

Spot him before you're hooked: Choose wisely whether to re-enter the rotation knowing your presence lasts only as long as he's content. He avoids confrontation and disappears when things sour, returning only when he desires. Refrain from giving space to a man who disregards your well-being, using women as toys. Once past him, never look back.

57

Mr. Gamer

Who he is: He is the average sleep-away-the-hours and play-video-games-all-day-long type of person. All his free time is spent on gaming. He plays seven days a week, from morning to the late hours of the night. He doesn't even give his date the bare minimum, but he'll do the opposite to the players of the game. He will compliment and even say "*I love you*" to the people he's playing with. Get used to screams into his mic at his friends! This is the guy who would rather spend money on a 65″ 4K TV, PS4 Pro, VR goggles, and a ton of games instead of a wedding!

How he'll lure you in: It is a treat when he joins you after his games. How nice to have a girlfriend who also plays games! At first, you share and enjoy gaming together. You can do co-op and talk about games. You hole up with snacks and beverages and game your day away. He even built your gaming PC for you as a gift.

Spot him before you're hooked: He won't let you win, but that's because you must learn to beat him first. Over time, you realize there is nothing much in this exchange for you. It's all about him and his gaming, he doesn't take you out from time to time, it's taking a toll on your dating life. If you were to get up and leave, he wouldn't notice. He is NOT able to balance his time with you and his obligations. Yet he wants uninterrupted game time. Stop putting up with the neglect and cut your losses, date with others who understand time management!

58

Mr. Social Media Butterfly

Who he is: He enjoys playing the field and having fun when he's online. He's active on social media. He likes pictures of random girls and hasn't yet unfriended his ex. He either avoids sending a friend request to you or posting any pictures with you in them. He is completely quiet about you. He's going to hide you as much as possible as he's dating someone else or has another committed partner.

How he'll lure you in: At first, he brings his best character to the table. He keeps the conversation going. He gives flowers, chocolates, surprising kisses, or whatever he finds that pleases you best. You become the center of gravity for him though you don't exist in his virtual world.

Spot him before you're hooked: He regularly uses social media. Deep down, you wish that he changes his Facebook status from single to 'in a relationship' and disclose your relationship status or post your pictures. You try to think he keeps his private life offline, and it isn't fair to project your expectations onto him. But it appears like he's hiding you altogether. He is purposely vague or only posts a very occasional picture while he is active. He turns off chats and untags himself in your posts. He does not open Instagram messages around you, he turns comments off. While he thinks he gets away with his sketchier behavior, you continue your dating funnel!

59

Mr. Crazy Stalker Type

Who he is: He is a love addict, who repeatedly becomes involved in intense, codependent relationships and turns into a crazy, insecure stalker who can't move on. You might have dated him in the past, had one date, or a few vague interactions. You find yourself running into him or hearing from him too frequently. He tries to figure out how to contact you either by physical presence, texting, social media, phone, even mail.

How he'll lure you in: He compliments you as if you're the greatest thing since sliced bread, without even knowing you. At first, he tries to address your emotional needs. He gets more possessive of you by the minute. He indulges his clingy, needy, selfish, scary obsession. He wants to learn every detail of your life. He stalks your social media pages to get more information about you. He likes everything you post and comments with inappropriate emojis as if he is in your inner circle of friends. He is consumed with you and your life.

Spot him before you're hooked: You feel on edge, he won't stop calling you after you ask him to stop or comes to your home or work uninvited. He does not respect your boundaries and clearly doesn't want to either. Stalking is the most dangerous form of obsession and may require a legal remedy. Your safety matters far more than his feelings. Obsessive behavior makes him high risk for violence and stalking. Don't underestimate the danger you could be in. Put your supports in place. Do so very carefully. Safety comes before all.

60

Mr. Closeted Man

Who he is: He is secretly attracted to men and hiding his true self. He remains closeted by having a nice woman on his shoulder in public who he can show off. He would in fact marry a woman as a cover up. He is a minefield of random quirks and desires. He could be romantically attracted to you, but only physically attracted to men, even with no romance involved. He enjoys random sexual preferences, and you're dreaming if you think that those preferences begin and end with you.

How he'll lure you in: He is an extremely good-looking man. He pays more attention to what makes a man attractive. No brainer, you are physically attracted to him. You interact more comfortably and intimately with him.

Spot him before you're hooked: Eventually, he won't be interested in sex with you. He never had any sincere sexual interest in you. But at first, you can't know from appearance, mannerisms, or fashion choices alone. You might notice that there are lots of different men on his social media profile. If you have suspicions, the beach vacation is usually a good way to sort this one out. He may try to catch a glimpse of other men and have prolonged eye contact with them. If he seems a little too eager to cuddle with his friends, or he is very keen on being naked around them, these are the red flags you should not ignore. You don't need to wait for him to come out, he may be relieved when you end things. Time to move on with your dating funnel.

61

Mr. Widower

Who he is: You are the love of his life after his wife died, though he is still grieving. He will have a meltdown on her birthday. He will have another meltdown on the 5th anniversary of her death. He has a few tattoos in honor of his late wife. You will be surrounded by photos of the late wife and wedding pictures. He feels guilty to his late wife's family and his children, and he won't post anything about you on social media, keeping you as a dirty little secret. He doesn't share any emotional intimacy with you and treats you like a rebound to meet his physical needs. He will make you feel like a placeholder instead of an actual girlfriend.

How he'll lure you in: Finding a connection remains a huge urge for him. The conversation flows easily, he is funny and interesting. His attention is flattering. You feel wanted and respected. His presence soothes you when nothing else could. You might sympathize with him and want to help him, knowing that he may value you for it.

Spot him before you're hooked: All of us grieve, in a way, for the rest of our lives after losing loved ones. It involves a great amount of mourning, healing, rebuilding, processing, and rediscovering that can linger for years. You must have compassion to be surrounded by other people's memories. A high value widower will get swooped up early on. But if your widower is unsure about you because he feels no one can replace his deceased wife, his children and family are not welcoming and are constantly comparing you to her, or if you feel you are just someone to fill the void and he is not ready to move forward, you need to let go of this one.

62

Mr. Promises The-Moon-In-Bed

Who he is: This is the man that your fun time just takes a sudden detour after he promises the moon to you in bed. He chooses to have self-conscious silence or avoids sex all together rather than have a direct conversation with honesty so that, as a couple, you can seek out a more flexible approach to sex. Knowing that he has options may reduce some of his performance pressure.

How he'll lure you in: He will lure you in with kisses and romantic dinners. He sets the mood talking about sex. You think he will send you to the moon and you will never come back… You get in a sexual mood, but he does not initiate sex.

Spot him before you're hooked: His difficulties can be very treatable for many and can be adapted to by most. If he is secure enough in himself to be honest with you and you are able to hear his honesty, then you can handle this situation well and you will then also be better able to handle all sorts of other situations well. If he does not have a good attitude and focuses on the success of the encounter that all hangs on his ability, then he is not going to make it easy for you. Resentment festering, frustration forming, or boredom start to take hold. Next is take the detour and continue on your dating funnel.

63

Mr. Clingy

Who he is: He is emotionally needy. He constantly needs to be reassured of your feelings for him and on the status of your relationship. His feelings are easily hurt when you go out with your girlfriends. When you're not with him, he's constantly blowing up your phone. He gets jealous easily, even if there isn't any reason for him to be. He has low self-esteem and is very insecure about who he is as a person.

How he'll lure you in: He is very attentive. He makes a supreme effort to see you. At first flattered, and then terrified, he wants to spend time and talk to you 24/7. He moves way too fast. You find him being the one and only.

Spot him before you're hooked: He lets go of his hobbies and interests. He does not have a life beyond you. He will stalk you on social media, hang around your favorite spots and follow you around. He won't hesitate to cross the line of your personal space. He expects you to text back immediately and gets mad when you go out without him. He doesn't trust you. He will blame you for his jealousy. He also expects similar clinginess from your side, but only to the point that he doesn't get annoyed. If you can't teach him "me" time, it's healthier for you to break up with him.

64

Mr. F-Boy

Who he is: He thinks he is god's gift to earth and is usually pretty damn beautiful. He only wants one thing, smoothing his way into your pants. He is self-absorbed, doesn't care for your emotions, and won't commit. He will likely cheat no matter what. He shares common traits with Mr. Ghoster, in fact he invented ghosting. When you start to get serious, he will ghost you. He is good at playing Peek-A-Boo. He will miraculously appear again when he needs to scratch the itch down there.

How he'll lure you in: Have you ever dated a guy you thought was the most thoughtful, romantic, and caring man, but also too touchy on the first date? His spontaneity opens you up to fun, joy, and happiness, but a short one… He will sweet talk you into having sex with him by getting to know your favorite things and get them for you. After he gets in your pants, he will stop doing all those nice things.

Spot him before you're hooked: He only compliments your good looks. He will talk about what he likes in bed. He wants to see you late at night. He hides his texts and lies about who he is with. He won't respect you, but will rely on you heavily. His ego can't handle being ignored. When you don't put his needs before yours, you are one step closer to mastering the art of ignoring him properly and moving on from the damaging on-again-off-again dynamic. Or he might dump you himself because he got bored of you. Save your dignity and run!

65

Mr. Proud-Of-His-Ex

Who he is: He speaks of his ex with so much love and enthusiasm. He keeps bringing up memories from the past. He blames himself for the end of the relationship. Even his therapist, his church counselor, and neighbors say so. Believe him. His toxic self chooses open, kind people with lavish hearts and he knows that very well. There is something wrong with him to leave a good wife.

How he'll lure you in: He makes you feel amazing. He will shower you with lavish gifts, flurry flowers, texts, and compliments. He is very attentive and affectionate. You are smitten by him. He seems like a perfect fictional boyfriend at first.

Spot him before you're hooked: He talks about her a lot in conversation and her name continuously comes up, along with things they did or shared together. He continues to act depressed about what went down between them, then rest assured, he hasn't put it behind him. At times, he might even compare you with her. Don't let his remorse and regret fill you with self-doubt. There will always be broken people, broken hearts, and broken relationships around him. Steer clear of him.

66

Mr. Holistic Vegan

Who he is: He is vegan. He has long hippie hair and wears rainbow-themed shirts. He spends hours meditating, doing his so called "spiritual work". He attends the hippy woo woo events and goes to wellness seminars. He is self-righteous, knows better than everyone. Food is just how he acts out. He lives on moral wellness on his spiritual journey. He is so involved and wise. He always gives unsolicited advice, how to be a more elevated person.

How he'll lure you in: You like his organic garden and enjoy his vegan dishes. You even like the smell of his natural deodorant. You are fine eating the black bean burger as long as he stays as sweet as he is.

Spot him before you're hooked: Your lifestyle choices are your own, not his. He needs to respect you and how you are. He will judge you, and his disapproval will annoy you. He will criticize your every meal and ultimately, each lifestyle choice you own. Even going vegetarian won't help. He'll regard that as just a first step to the ultimate goal, his way, or the highway. Please choose the highway and get yourself a big juicy burger!

67

Mr. Sugar Daddy

Who he is: He will win you over with his money and gifts. He is old, unattractive, and married. He will throw gifts, allowances, and trips in exchange of friendship, maybe even more… He feels good about himself when he constantly gives, and you are the receiver. He feels powerful since he sets the boundaries and expectations. The financial nature of sugar dating helps him feel more secure about his dating relationships. He is regaining his past in the company of a younger woman who looks up to him.

How he'll lure you in: He is very well-motivated to keep you happy. He needs his ego stroked to the point that he offers you financial incentives to stay with him. You might hesitate at first, but could actually be impressed by the expensive piece of jewelry he bought for your birthday.

Spot him before you're hooked: If he is showering you with cash, gifts, and prizes like you just won the Wheel of Fortune, stay away from this man. He can be toxic, and you could subject yourself to sexual violence. He is not doing charity or is not troubled with having so much money, he is just making an investment and wants a payback, just in a different currency. He expects sex, good acting, and fake devotion. Run!

68

Mr. Split-The-Check

Who he is: He always goes "Dutch" when on dates with women. If she offers to pay or split the check on a date, he will take the offer graciously. He rushes on dates. He may go to the restaurant earlier and already ordered his plate or he is only interested in a drink. He may ask to split the dish because he does not eat much, or he is on a diet. He will make you feel obligated to treat him when you are out together. He usually dates just long enough to get "paid some other way" and then moves along to his next adventure.

How he'll lure you in: He is courting you and making plans, following up, asking questions about you, and says he wants to take you out on a date. He may even start creating a romantic fantasy via text that will allow you to feel like you're more romantically connected than he's earned by actually taking you out on dates. By the time he sees you, you feel like you've already been dating for weeks. He can easily ask for splitting the check or act like you are roommates on your first date.

Spot him before you're hooked: Don't rely on your date paying, as some men, despite initiating, may expect to split the check, signaling potential reluctance for long-term commitment. Ensure he values your time over financial dynamics; consider suggesting cost-sharing or affordable alternatives. If his approach doesn't align with your relationship expectations, move on to the next in your funnel.

69

Mr. Ethically Non-Monogamous

Who he is: He either discloses that he is ethically non-monogamous (ENM) in his dating profile or later after a few conversations or you will figure it out. If he discloses in his profile, he is at least not wasting anyone's time who isn't like minded. By declaring ENM, he is practicing taking part in romantic relationships that are not completely exclusive between two people and he is seeking women who consent to it.

How he'll lure you in: He is capable of loving multiple women at once and feels more satisfied in life when he is able to do that. He is relaxed. He believes ENM isn't cheating because both you and him have agreed in advance that you'll be practicing non-monogamy. You're attracted to his honesty and confidence. He is strong willed and knows what he wants in life. It might be hard stepping back once either of you has confessed your love.

Spot him before you're hooked: What is the point of liking his profile and message him if you're clearly not into that lifestyle? You're probably going to catch feelings if you decide to meet him, and he is still the same person. There are men out there who want to be invested in one woman and exclusively date you. Don't forget that you have a funnel with men that their ultimate goal is to be exclusive with one woman.

70

Mr. Polyamorous

Who he is: He is already in a relationship and has numerous partners. He uses the labels of "polyamorous" and "ENM" as an excuse for flat-out terrible behavior. He will use polyamory to excuse cheating, then dupe his partners into thinking that it's okay. He will force double standards on you, while he can pursue outside romantic and/or emotional connections with others.

How he'll lure you in: He will lure you in his connected polyamorous network. He will act all too sweet and show you the brighter side. He makes you believe how talented he is to treat all his partners equally. He might promise to never emotionally abuse you because of his other partners, but know that it's all a lie. He is in a long-term commitment to more than one person simultaneously.

Spot him before you're hooked: He will dupe you into thinking you are dating one person, and then rope you into a surprise couple date. He will inform you of secret rules he has established with you and his other partners. He will deliberately instigate fights between his partners for his personal entertainment. He will demand that you must befriend or spend time with his partner. Don't put any emotional investment into a relationship with this type of man. He has a lot of time in his hands and uses women for entertainment. He is totally selfish and passive-aggressive, leading you to feel guilty for even going out with your friends. Run!

71

Mr. Simpleton

Who he is: He is kind and a sweet guy, but does not stimulate you mentally or romantically. He is resistant to new ideas or experiences and unwilling to engage in deeper discussions or exploration of new topics. To take it to the next level, you constantly keep feeling like something is missing. He is naive, gullible, or slow-witted. He lacks drive and motivation in his personal and professional life, leading you to feel uninspired or unimpressed.

How he'll lure you in: Even if he doesn't feel like the most interesting or intelligent person in the world, he owns who he is and what he brings to the table. He is a good listener. He shows genuine interest in what you have to say. He kind of seems cute to you so you may find him attractive.

Spot him before you're hooked: He lacks passion and excitement in his interests and conversations, leaving you feeling disengaged and uninterested. He lacks the personality traits that you find appealing in a romantic partner. He may struggle to understand or empathize with your feelings and needs, making it difficult to build emotional intimacy and connection. You will eventually be bored and keep feeling lonely as always. Choose to move on.

Mr. Fetish

Who he is: He's got a foot fetish, he's got eyes for your slender, freshly painted toes. But that is probably not the only thing he is attracted to, he could be into kinks like BDSM (bondage, domination, submission, and masochism), cross-dressing, voyeurism, and exhibitionism. He may be into role-playing, and various forms of sensory plays for sexual stimulation. On his online profile, he may be dressed up as a woman. He seeks like-minded individuals who may be open to exploring fetishes and kinks.

How he'll lure you in: He has this keen interest in exploring new sensual activities and you might enjoy the adventures that are new to you. He will watch the Fifty Shades of Grey with you for the 100th time. His comments about how sexy you are or how much he wants you are flattering and makes you feel good. His kisses are long, passionate, and lingering.

Spot him before you're hooked: Fetishes are a normal and healthy part of human sexuality, and people have a wide range of different fetishes and sexual preferences. As long as all sexual activities are consensual, safe, and legal, there is no "right" or "wrong" way to express one's sexuality. Learn about the extent of his fetish, and if you're not cool with what he's into, say so. You should never do something you really don't want to do, regardless of how much you care about someone. If you just can't handle his fetish, that's a perfectly good reason to part ways.

73

Mr. Glued-To-His-Phone

Who he is: He is simply addicted to his phone or social media and has a hard time disconnecting. He constantly checks on his phone. He answers his phone while on a date and does not even have the curtesy to say, "Sorry, I have to take this." Or give some explanation. It is difficult to have a meaningful conversation or to feel like you have their undivided attention.

How he'll lure you in: Sparks fly on virtual dates, but not so much in real life. When sending text messages, he uses a mix of emojis, GIFs, and memes to convey his emotions and add personality to his messages. He is quick to respond to messages and enjoys keeping up an ongoing dialogue throughout the day. He prefers texting over phone calls or in person conversations. You are attracted to his cute text messages and attention.

Spot him before you're hooked: His smartphone will never leave his side. Dating a man who is glued to his phone can be frustrating and can make you feel neglected. Let him know how his behavior is affecting you and try to find a compromise that works for both of you. You could establish phone-free times during your dates or set boundaries around phone use when you're spending time together. If he is unwilling to make changes or compromises, it may be a sign that he is not as invested. In that case, it may be best to reassess whether the relationship is right for you and continue on with your dating funnel.

Mr. Misogynist

Who he is: He holds a deep-seated dislike, contempt, or prejudice towards women. He believes that men are superior to women and that women are meant to be subservient to men. He uses derogatory language and make comments that undermine women's intelligence, abilities, or worth. He blames women for problems or issues that are not their fault or hold them responsible for negative consequences that result from his own actions.

How he'll lure you in: He uses charm, flattery, or other manipulative tactics to get what he wants from you. At first, he demonstrates empathy and support. He might look like a very mature and intellectual individual. He seems as if he is able to understand and relate to your needs and concerns.

Spot him before you're hooked: He dismisses your opinions and experiences and refuses to engage in constructive dialogue with you. He views women solely as sexual objects and makes inappropriate comments and gestures. He tries to control you by dictating how you dress, who you spend time with, or what activities you engage in. He has a harmful and toxic mindset that can have serious consequences for your mental and physical wellbeing. Prioritize your safety and well-being and move on!

75

Mr. Dog Parent

Who he is: He is a dedicated dog parent, who has a strong bond with his dog(s). He plays, and snuggles with his dogs, and may even celebrate his dogs' birthdays or other milestones. He typically views his dog(s) as members of his family and may treat them with the same level of care, affection, and attention that they would a human child. If you want to date this man, you must love dogs - all sizes, shapes, colors, and genders!

How he'll lure you in: When a man takes care of a dog, it shows that he has a nurturing side and is responsible. This can be a very attractive quality in a partner. You go for walks, runs, and hikes with his furry friend and enjoy nature more often.

Spot him before you're hooked: He prioritizes his dogs' needs above his own and yours. He has less flexibility in his schedule, as he needs to be available to take care of his dogs' needs, such as walking, feeding, and playing. He needs to budget for food, supplies, and veterinary care, which could affect his ability to go on expensive dates or travel. He deeply loves his furry friends and shows them affection through cuddles, playtime, and verbal praise. You will find out whether dogs feel jealousy when you start dating him. If you have pet allergies, dating him could be challenging, as you may need to avoid spending time in his home or with his dog. If you are not a dog person, or if your personality or lifestyle does not mesh well with the dogs' temperament or energy level, this could cause issues. Think more practically.

76

Mr. Cat Lover

Who he is: He is a cat lover. He talks to his cat, cuddles with his cat, or even takes his cat with him on outings. You always come in second to his cat. He cancels plans or stays home more often to be with his cat, and he prioritizes spending time with his cat over spending time with you.

How he'll lure you in: He has a creative or artistic side that he enjoys expressing. You both enjoy creative activities such as writing, drawing, or playing music. He is affectionate and caring, and he values physical touch and intimacy in his relationships.

Spot him before you're hooked: If you're not a cat person yourself, you may find it hard to relate to his love for his cat. You may view cat ownership as feminine or emasculating, which can create tension and insecurity in your relationship. Even if you don't have allergies yourself, spending time in a cat-filled environment can cause discomfort and make it hard for you to enjoy spending time together. He prefers to spend more time at home with his cat, rather than going out and being social. This can lead to conflicts if you have different expectations. If you can't overcome these obstacles, keep building your funnel and seek building a strong, fulfilling relationship with a man who does not have a feline companion.

77

Mr. Serial Slob

Who he is: His home is cluttered and disorganized, which makes it difficult to spend time together or invite friends over. He is isolated and struggles with socializing or maintaining relationships. He intends to clean his car or house, but simply never gets around to it. He procrastinates or puts off tasks that are not immediately important or urgent. He is comfortable with filth.

How he'll lure you in: He remembers important details about you and surprises you with small gestures of kindness, like bringing you your favorite coffee, wearing your favorite color, or leaving a thoughtful note for you. He likes being domestic with you. He's certainly interested in being comfortable at your house, not his.

Spot him before you're hooked: You won't be invited to his apartment or his house. He will always come to your place, leaving a trail behind him. He is capable, but is just taking the easy route, simply laying back letting you clean it. This can be a source of frustration or embarrassment if you are someone who values cleanliness and order. Save your sanity while it is salvageable. There is a guy out there for you who values a nice, clean home and will keep it tidy.

78

Mr. His-Ex-Wife-Cheated

Who he is: He initiates a conversation by presenting himself as a victim of his ex-wife's infidelity, highlighting his own virtues in the relationship. However, upon further investigation, it becomes clear that he is the one who drove his wife to cheat. If you give him a chance to share his side of the story, you will likely discover why his ex-wife sought comfort outside of the relationship.

How he'll lure you in: It appears that he has gained valuable insights from his past relationship and has become more self-aware and emotionally mature. He presents himself in a way that implies he was the more mature partner in his previous relationship. He plays the victim of his ex's cheating plot against him and how he was totally devastated and shattered because he had put all his best and sincere efforts in their precious-to-him relationship. You develop a sense of empathy towards his story and feel attracted towards his sincerity.

Spot him before you're hooked: You feel emotionally ignored, undervalued, and sexually unsatisfied. You start feeling disconnected from him. This disconnection causes you to seek validation or emotional connection from someone else. Similar to his ex-wife, you begin experiencing personal challenges, such as feelings of low self-worth or symptoms of depression. To avoid finding yourself in this predicament, it's important to continue using your dating funnel to seek out someone who values and respects you.

79

Mr. Bookworm

Who he is: He prioritizes his reading and intellectual pursuits over spending quality time with you. He is so engrossed in his books that he forgets to engage with you or neglects to take care of his own chores. He spends hours reading or researching, even when you are trying to spend time with him, leading to feelings of frustration and isolation.

How he'll lure you in: He is intellectually stimulating. You both enjoy a certain genre of books or have a favorite author in common. He is proud of your interests and shows enthusiasm when you talk about your favorite books and authors. You also like to share common interests and are attracted to the silent connection you feel with him.

Spot him before you're hooked: He is emotionally distant and lacks the communication skills needed to connect with you on a deeper level. He struggles to balance his love for books with his love for you, and this imbalance can lead to relationship issues. Overall, while being a bookworm is not necessarily a negative trait, it can become problematic if it leads to neglecting you and neglecting the relationship. If he is obsessed with books and only books, you will definitely need to move on with the funnel.

80

Mr. Shakespeare-In-Love

Who he is: He is a romantic at heart, and enjoys expressing his feelings through poetry or other forms of art. He has a deep appreciation for Shakespeare's plays and sonnets and may see them as a source of inspiration for his own creative pursuits. He tends to be overly emotional. You will inevitably find that he's overly dramatic.

How he'll lure you in: Like Shakespeare, he has a keen sense of observation and an intense desire to understand human nature. He has a way with words that is very appealing to you at first. He uses his poetic abilities to express his feelings and shows his affection. This includes writing love poems, sending thoughtful messages, or planning romantic dates.

Spot him before you're hooked: He love-bombs with excessive flattery, affection, gifts, and attention to create a false sense of intimacy and connection, and then withdraws it suddenly as a way to manipulate and control you. He continues with drama despite your communication. You try to set some boundaries - this involves limiting your time with him, avoiding certain topics of conversation, or avoiding certain social situations. It's important to prioritize your own mental health and well-being. If his drama is causing you undue stress or anxiety, it's okay to distance yourself from him and focus on spending time with other dates who bring positivity and joy to your life.

81

Mr. Snapchat

Who he is: He enjoys staying in touch with friends and family through Snapchat, using the app to share pictures, videos, and messages. He regularly updates his Instagram feed, post stories, and counts his followers. He is very active in creating and posting content, and also enjoys interacting with others by commenting on or liking their posts.

How he'll lure you in: He flirts with you using Snapchat. He compliments on your pictures. He continually repeats how attractive you are because of those pictures. You send little jokes to each other. And the constant social media connection and attention from him makes you think about him more often.

Spot him before you're hooked: He only communicates with you on Snapchat. If you only see what he posts to his story, you're basically just like everyone else. He just wants attention and will accept it from everyone, *not just you*. He expects you to send him sexy snaps all the time in place of having an intellectual conversation. You deserve to be permanent in someone's life, and not have them disappear like a ghost in less than ten seconds with the swift motion of a thumb.

82

Mr. Conspiracy Theorist

Who he is: He's immersed in conspiracy theories and misinformation, avidly exploring TikTok trends and viral videos. His interests range from UFOs to paranormal phenomena. Be prepared for intense conversations on topics like midterm elections or the origins of the coronavirus.

How he'll lure you in: After months of swiping, you are surprised to meet someone so seemingly lovely and normal who is communicative and committed. He is very attentive. He enjoys engaging in deep discussions and debates about controversial topics. You like the fact that he is very passionate about his beliefs and opinions until you get the hint of that nonsense—totally kills the vibe.

Spot him before you're hooked: His interest in conspiracy theories is negatively impacting his mental health, causing him to feel anxious or paranoid about the world around him. He lets conspiracy theories consume his thoughts and actions. It can be very upsetting to hear him say things that seem to you like obvious, falsifiable nonsense. To him, these beliefs bring a sense of belonging, control, and even entertainment. Please use your judgement to determine if he's getting too far into something that is actually dangerous. Run!

83

Mr. Pilot

Who he is: You will be bread crumbed by a pilot and he won't respond to your last text. He will cancel a date with you an hour before you were going to meet. Blame it on jet lag or being on call. He will be gone for days at a time, but he will figure out how to keep seeing you. He will request a layover in your hometown again next week! You won't like the warm/cold you get from him. He would regularly cheat on his wife and tell you he is separated.

How he'll lure you in: He has stories to tell from all over the world. He is open minded. He will always share what he is drinking or eating in photos in exotic places, like Paris or European cities, he flies to. He gives the anticipation to you that one day you will go to these romantic places together.

Spot him before you're hooked: You don't want to unfairly judge him by his profession, because there are a lot of stereotypes surrounding pilots such as sleeping with flight attendants, napping in cockpits, having kids in every city and high divorce rate aka AIDS – Aviation Induced Divorce Syndrome. He could very well be a high value man. You just have to make sure that he is the one. How you proceed thereafter requires insight and preparation. Dating a pilot can be hard since they are often away and can't be contacted easily. To survive dating a pilot, you need to be independent. If this is a deal-breaker for you, then you should not get into the relationship and save everyone a lot of tears.

Mr. Avoidant

Who he is: He has a deep-seated fear of emotional intimacy. He struggles to express his emotions or connect with you. He is dismissive of your needs or feelings, which can create feelings of rejection and hurt. He is hesitant to commit to a long-term relationship or has a history of avoiding commitment altogether.

How he'll lure you in: He remembers how you like your coffee or what your favorite dessert is; it's a sign he cares about you. He'll flirt with you, tease you, and even lightly touch you. He's one of the cute types and seem too attractive to let go.

Spot him before you're hooked: He needs a lot of personal space and time alone, which can be confusing or hurtful to you. He pulls away emotionally when you become too close. He prioritizes his own independence and self-reliance over your needs. He is distrustful of others. He shows physical affection only during sex. When you most need him, he will find ways not to be there. He will stonewall when you want to address relationship issues. Do NOT rush into an exclusive relationship with this man, he will leave you feeling emotionally deprived.

85

Mr. History Buff

Who he is: He will be "obsessing" about your relationship history, even after you have detailed it in full. He not only talks about them, but wants to dive deep with you investigating the reasoning behind them. He has insecurities. He has the urge to explore every past event in your life.

How he'll lure you in: His obsession in your relationship history is a conversation starter. He asks questions, circulating conversation around you. You share your vulnerable stories and intimate details about your life. You have hopes you will be cultivating a great relationship with him through a lot of understanding and bonding.

Spot him before you're hooked: He puts off important conversations in favor of learning more about your relationship history. He expresses insecurity and doubt. He is quite fixated on what you have done before he came along. Mature, confident men don't worry about what happened before they got together with you. He would be focused on what is going on right now and what they are going to make happen in the future. If he gets too ridiculous, please go on dates with men who have better sense.

86

Mr. Clueless

Who he is: He is clueless about dating to a level you have to teach him how to ask you out. He asks you to come over to his place on the first date. He thinks hanging out is going on a date. You are patient and understanding as you guide him through the process. You think it's possible that he simply lacks experience or confidence in dating.

How he'll lure you in: He stares at you... a lot. He talks to you all the time on social media, but has a hard time doing it in person. He is really sweet, but quiet while around you. He lingers around you just because he feels comfortable and safe around you. He also will be very nervous to make any physical moves until certain you like him back.

Spot him before you're hooked: His confused personality will never allow him to properly commit to you. Even if he does commit to you somehow, he may change his mind later. He doesn't even know if he likes you or not. If he thinks that hanging out is a date, be clear about what you want. Let him know that you're interested in going on a real date and suggest a specific activity or location. You would let him know that it would be welcome if he asked you. From courting to marriage, a doubt shouldn't be in your head. If you feel like you've sent the message loud and clear to your preferences and he acts like either he didn't hear or doesn't care, it is time to move on.

87

Mr. Celebrity

Who he is: You are valid with your concerns. He may swap out girlfriends for younger model looks. He may be looking for an easy hookup because you are a fan. Your personal life may be in the public eye, and you may be followed by paparazzi or interviewed by the media. He often has a busy schedule due to work commitments, and this can make it challenging to spend time together.

How he'll lure you in: Despite any differences in fame, he makes you feel valued and respected. He doesn't think you're a groupie or a crazy stalker fan. Besides, you get to hear his music before anyone else!

Spot him before you're hooked: Celebrities live on a different planet to the rest of us — and go by different rules. It's important to maintain a sense of equality in the relationship. You may have to deal with rumors or accusations of infidelity or be subjected to scrutiny from fans or the media. It's important to establish trust early on and be honest. Have a conversation with him about how much you're comfortable sharing and establish boundaries around your privacy. If dating a celebrity gets overwhelming, you can filter him out and continue on your dating funnel!

88

Mr. Obsessed with Cars

Who he is: Obsessed with cars, he dedicates nearly 100% of his time to the shop, racing, and car-related activities. With multiple vehicles and midnight purchases of expensive parts, his spending and time commitment becomes a source of resentment, making you resentful towards his cars and racing buddies.

How he'll lure you in: He shows up in a fancy car to your date. He constantly bombards you with messages and sends pictures of his rides. Cars have been his favorite make-out location since they started rolling out of the factories. Luckily, you don't have to go on a long trip to have fun or feel the romance blossom between the two of you. Instead, you can have some of the most sensuous moments in his parked car. You get fascinated by the idea of dating in a new car every day.

Spot him before you're hooked: He acts like a teenager. Making out in a car is one of the oldest pastimes bringing up memories of his teenage years. He moves too quickly in physical intimacy or pushes for exclusivity too soon. Overdoing it early in dating is off putting and overwhelming for you. The relationship gets boring for you because there's only one new thing in the relationship every day: a different car. You question if cars turn him on more than you do.

89

Mr. Sperm Donor

Who he is: He dates with no strings attached, engages in casual sexual relationships with women, and he does not take the legal steps to establish paternity with any of the resulting children. He does not pursue a committed or long-term relationship with the mothers with any expectation of co-parenting. He will be at risk of being held responsible for financial or legal obligations related to the children.

How he'll lure you in: He is persistent. He is possessive of you very early on. He claims you instantly. He will be on his sneaky best behavior until you let your guard down.

Spot him before you're hooked: The best predictor of future behavior is past behavior, and his past behavior is a huge red flag. He obviously doesn't use protection. He has a complete lack of responsibility when it comes to reproductive health. If you plan well and think about these things beforehand, you will wait till you are in a stable committed relationship to have children. It is important to consider the future potential legal, emotional, and health risks involved dating this type of man and getting into a casual sexual relationship. You may not have any legal protection or recourse if complications arise. Getting into a relationship with this man is no different than entering into a donor arrangement. Run!

Mr. Shy Guy

Who he is: He is super shy. He is scared about how to ask out a girl and what to do once he is out and about with you. He won't come forward. You have to take a chance and ask him out. You don't get to choose if you're on the passive end. If you go out with him, you should have been named the Shy Guys' Mentor of the Year.

How he'll lure you in: He intrigues you and you go for it! You'd rather date an attractive shy guy who's intelligent, and has ambition, over many of the 'low-quality guys' who frequently approach you. He gets red in the face and blushes around you. He hints a million different ways about how he wants to do something with you, but won't be blunt about it either.

Spot him before you're hooked: Since he is shy, you choose less stressful dates than a formal date. His silence and fear could be emotionally and mentally exhausting for you. Lack of expression from his side will soon make you frustrated. If you don't like his ways and the way he handles things without trying to shape him into someone he's not, he's not the guy for you.

91

Mr. Social Climber

Who he is: He uses you only to advance his own career prospects or to become the new popular kid in town. Are you a popular girl with a lot of friends? Or are you working somewhere influential and have a lot of powerful friends? You'd definitely be on his dating list since he could benefit from the people you know.

How he'll lure you in: He is charming and charismatic and tries to win you over by flattering you or offering you something in return for your connections. He's very professional and knows how to work his words. He shows a sudden interest in your social or professional circle.

Spot him before you're hooked: He will exploit your connections for his own gain, such as using them to advance his career or social status. He prefers meeting you when your friends are around. He loves going to social gatherings with you. He likes public dates more than a romantic twosome date. He is motivated by his own self-interest rather than genuine connection and friendship. He is quick to ask for favors or introductions without offering anything in return. Avoid him because he'll squeeze you dry and walk all over you once he's got what he wanted.

Mr. Anxious

Who he is: He will seek constant reassurance from you to alleviate his anxiety, which can be emotionally draining for you. He worries about rejection which leads to clinginess and jealousy. He constantly sows doubt and confusion. He overthinks and analyzes every aspect of the relationship, which can lead to feelings of anxiety and stress.

How he'll lure you in: At first, he is authentic and true to himself, and lets his unique qualities shine through. His difficulty communicating his feelings and needs creates misunderstandings and conflicts.

Spot him before you're hooked: He avoids activities that trigger his anxiety. This limits the opportunities for shared experiences and growth while dating. Sometimes anxious thoughts, feelings of inadequacy and self-doubt motivate him to act in ways that stress you out and strain the relationship. He feels insecure about his worth and value, which leads to insults, accusations, and threats. Stay positive and focus on your personal growth and self-improvement. It can be overwhelming to you because you're not the professional therapist he needs. Give him space to heal and move on.

93

Mr. Beta Male

Who he is: He struggles with making decisions or taking initiative. He relies on you to take the lead. He is passive or avoidant in conflict. It is hard to address issues and resolve disagreements, which creates imbalance or resentment over time.

How he'll lure you in: At first, you like the fact that he prioritizes harmony and cooperation in his relationships. Then you realize he struggles with confidence and self-esteem, which affects his ability to express himself or take risks in the relationship.

Spot him before you're hooked: He defers to you for guidance. You have a hard time finding common ground or meeting his needs, because of his lack of expression, which is the most important part of any relationship. This can make it challenging to build intimacy or trust over time. You may find that his more passive or cooperative approach is not a good match for you. Better be more practical and wish him luck for his complicated love life while you move on.

94

Mr. Alpha Male

Who he is: He competes with you for control of the relationship. He prioritizes logic and reason over empathy and understanding, making it hard to connect emotionally. He has a hard time admitting when he is wrong. He has difficulty expressing his emotions or communicating his needs and feelings. He has a demanding career that makes it challenging to find time to connect.

How he'll lure you in: He is a bicep-bulging, beer-toting, scruffy-looking alpha male. He is the manly man, who has a more primal *if not cave man* appeal. He is confident, assertive, and dominant. His strong personality is both attractive and intimidating.

Spot him before you're hooked: Dating an alpha male can be both exciting and challenging. He won't want to watch chick flicks with you, or ten minutes in, would start complaining about the dozens of clothes you're trying on just looking for "the dress." It becomes challenging to resolve conflicts and move past disagreements with him. He has a dominant character and struggles with compromise or collaboration. This can lead to power struggles and difficulties finding common ground. You may encounter conflicts every day around every single thing you do together. Choose your mental peace over a man and move on.

95

Mr. Has-A-Jealous-Daughter

Who he is: He has a manipulative daughter who is openly greedy, jealous, and mean. She has Daddy wrapped around her finger. She draws him back with "I don't want to share my daddy" with you. She seems to resent everything you do and makes it her mission to ruin any chance of happiness your relationship might have. You feel guilty for thinking that his daughter could possibly be purposefully malicious, but it often feels that way. You're feeling ignored when the daughter is around. You are unsure how to approach the situation with him, since he needs to set and enforce boundaries for his daughter.

How he'll lure you in: You're attracted to his responsible and nurturing nature. You like the fact that he is actively involved in his kids' lives - giving love support and guidance. You think this is great news for you. A responsible father - that's a much rarer creature!

Spot him before you're hooked: He does NOT express to his daughter his interest and love for you. He keeps his dating life separate from his daughter. He allows his daughter to dominate him. He ostracizes you for entire weekends until his time with his daughter is up and she goes back with the ex-wife. In relationships, you should not feel like anyone else comes first. It should be an integrated part of living, growing, learning, and having a good life. If you don't like to be in this situation, then move on to someone who is more available without kids or has kids but is a dad who is more autonomous and free thinking.

96

Mr. Entrepreneur

Who he is: He pretends to be an entrepreneur, but is actually broke. He tries to impress you or others by portraying himself as an entrepreneur on his online dating profile. He doesn't possess the two crucial qualities of an entrepreneur - ambition and drive. You may start to wonder if he's being honest with you about other aspects of his life.

How he'll lure you in: He has a mature look and a gentleman-like personality. He attracts you with his confidence, charisma, and unique passion that sets him apart as an entrepreneur. This is inspiring and motivating for you and creates a sense of shared ambition and excitement about your future together.

Spot him before you're hooked: He is not good at managing his finances. You may find yourself picking up the tab more often or covering expenses that he can't afford. He is not as interested in going on vacations, buying a house, or saving for retirement, which can create tension and resentment over time if those are things that are important to you. It may lead to trust issues. It's important to prioritize your own needs and happiness. So, do both of you a favor and cut your losses and move on sooner rather than later.

97

Mr. Flirt

Who he is: He flirts with every woman in his vicinity while you are present. He flirts with bank clerks, waitresses, cashiers, which creates an awkward or uncomfortable dynamic between the two of you.

How he'll lure you in: He is confident and outgoing and enjoys the attention and excitement that comes with flirting with others. At first, you find his behavior charming or flattering, and see it as harmless fun. Though, later his flirts turn into toxic, unwanted advances which lead to awkward and uncomfortable situations.

Spot him before you're hooked: He flirts excessively and inappropriately. He only knows how to communicate through flirting. He struggles to form genuine connections. He's trying to provoke a jealous reaction with his playful and suggestive language; it backfires with you. You perceive him as unprofessional and disrespectful. Eventually, you will conclude that he's not mature enough to be a good boyfriend, and certainly, not your boyfriend.

Mr. Interrogator

Who he is: He is a pushy person. He texts you multiple times a day and wants to talk every day before you meet. You feel like you are being interrogated so he could tick off a list. He asks too many questions. He becomes overfamiliar and conversations get deeper than you would want. He interferes in all your personal matters to the point of controlling you.

How he'll lure you in: You feel very flattered as he is putting in so much effort pursuing you. He is assertive and proactive in pursuing you to a level that you try to slow him down without turning him off or him switching the leading on to you.

Spot him before you're hooked: You feel pushed and annoyed with him not listening to you or trying to find a way to change your mind. The intensity of his pursuit seems disproportionate. Even though you like him, you feel like you can't get to know him because you spend the whole time having to shield yourself. There is no personal space for you because he does not respect boundaries at all. You feel like prey, not a person. Wish him the best in love and move on!

99

Mr. Fast and Furious

Who he is: He is focused on action and adventure. He takes risks or pushes himself to his limits in pursuit of his goals. He struggles with commitment, as he prefers the thrill of the chase over settling down with one person.

How he'll lure you in: He is spontaneous, adventurous, creative, and fun-loving. There is no dull moment with him. If you're open to new experiences and enjoy spontaneity, you may find it exciting and refreshing to be around him. He does things on a whim, which can be exciting but also potentially dangerous.

Spot him before you're hooked: He does not like to plan ahead. It is difficult to know what to expect from him or plan activities together. He acts without thinking things through or considering the consequences. This can lead to impulsive and often irrational decisions that can be difficult to handle. He enjoys taking risks and pushing boundaries. He puts you in uncomfortable or risky situations. You might have to look after things in your work schedule, but that could cause him to be upset. A life without a schedule is unstable. You are searching for the high value man who brings structure and predictability in your life, Mr. Fast and Furious won't.

100

Mr. Passport Bro

Who he is: He seeks a "traditional wife" overseas. He is not interested in your education, personality, or other traits, but rather your submission to him. He thinks he can increase his odds of staying married or stay in a relationship if he is with a foreign woman or a woman born abroad.

How he'll lure you in: He idolizes you from afar for your exotic looks. He likes the attention he is getting. He glorifies you and he is ready to spoil you. He is expressive and acts all too sweet around you. He puts in efforts that seem genuine to maintain stability in the relationship. He apologizes easily and doesn't let you stay mad for a long time. You also enjoy the cultural differences and curiously want to explore his side of the world, along with his sweet and caring nature.

Spot him before you're hooked: His needs in a partner are less basic or survivor based. He will not like if you challenge his authority. He is anti-feminist. He objectifies women and reduces them to stereotypes. You will be shocked to find just how much stereotyping in his conversations is directed at both western and eastern women. Stereotypes are not always true. The key in dating is to strike a balance between acknowledging the importance of culture while recognizing the unique qualities of each individual. If your date treats you as a unique individual, with your own beliefs, values, and experiences rather than assuming that you fit into a particular stereotype, he is a keeper! If he is seeking out relationships based on stereotypes, you should RUN!

101

Mr. High Value

Who he is: He has clarity around his mission, purpose, and direction. He has his life and finances in order. He has strong sense of integrity, values, and honor. He is open minded, curious, and revels in the beauty and mystery of life. He knows how to give and earn respect.

How he'll lure you in: He is open, honest, and vulnerable. He welcomes and actively creates deep emotional intimacy. He listens well and remembers what you say. He is charismatic, confident, and fun to be around. He stands up for himself, for you, and for your relationship.

Spot him before you're hooked: He sees the incredible value that a good woman like you brings into his life. He respects and expresses gratitude in various healthy ways. He offers freely without expecting anything in return. He is not afraid to say no or assert himself. He is familiar with challenges and does not shy away. He is committed to inner work and personal development. He is supportive to your goals and respects your decisions. If you are able to spot this man and you two have an incredible chemistry, do NOT let him go!

ENGAGE WITH ESRA OZ

I would like to thank all of you for purchasing my book. I would love to hear from you on how you experienced *"Dating Funnel for Women: How to Spot Bad Boys and Filter Them Out Quickly; 100 Types of Men to Avoid."* If you are wanting to go deeper in your courageous work in dating, you can find my *Dating Funnel Journal* on Amazon. With this journal, you can now collect and refine all of your mindful observations for identifying and avoiding the types of men who are not worth your time. Keeping a journal reminds you of your progress and recognize types of men you should avoid who will break your heart, waste your years, and make you miss opportunities with the high value man you wish would love you and commit to you.

You can also join my social media community **"Dating Funnel for Women"** on Facebook and/or Instagram. Look for tips on dating and how to create a dating funnel. I look forward to having you join me.

Dating Funnel for Women Podcast

For more tips on how to date with more intention and less stress, listen to my podcast **"Dating Funnel for Women"** on Spotify and Apple Podcast. I also offer live group coaching on a rotating schedule and 1:1 coaching. Check out the website **www.datingfunnelforwomen.com** to see when the next session begins, explore the master class, and download a dating funnel blueprint as a reference for your dating journey and follow me on Instagram **@dresraoz**.

https://esraozdenerol.com/

https://www.datingfunnelforwomen.com/

www.ingramcontent.com/pod-product-compliance
Lightning Source LLC
Chambersburg PA
CBHW072029290326
41934CB00012BA/3145